WiX Cookbook

Over 60 hands-on recipes packed with tips and tricks to boost your Windows installations

Nick Ramirez

[PACKT] open source*
PUBLISHING   community experience distilled

BIRMINGHAM - MUMBAI

WiX Cookbook

First published: January 2015

Production reference: 1230115

Published by Packt Publishing Ltd.
Livery Place
35 Livery Street
Birmingham B3 2PB, UK.

ISBN 978-1-78439-321-2

www.packtpub.com

Credits

Author
Nick Ramirez

Reviewers
Jiří Činčura
Chris Eelmaa
Christopher Painter
Ranjith Sundarrajan

Commissioning Editor
Amarabha Banerjee

Acquisition Editor
Owen Roberts

Content Development Editor
Susmita Sabat

Technical Editors
Shiny Poojary
Sebastian Rodrigues

Copy Editors
Roshni Banerjee
Pranjali Chury
Puja Lalwani
Gladson Monteiro
Jasmine Nadar
Adithi Shetty

Project Coordinator
Milton Dsouza

Proofreaders
Ameesha Green
Elinor Perry-Smith
Jonathan Todd

Indexer
Tejal Soni

Production Coordinator
Shantanu N. Zagade

Cover Work
Shantanu N. Zagade

About the Author

Nick Ramirez is a software developer living in Columbus, Ohio. As a believer that deployment shouldn't be terrifying, he has become a big fan of technologies such as WiX. His other related interests include build automation, software architecture, and playing Minecraft. Nick lives with his wife and two cats.

I would like to thank the editors at Packt Publishing for making the process of writing so much easier. They are superb at keeping things on track and well organized. A big thanks goes to all those involved in the WiX community for continuing to pour vitality into the project and keeping the discussions going. There are many tireless volunteers who are always there to answer a question or start a discussion. Those developers who contribute source code to the WiX project deserve an extra bit of thanks for the hard work that they do. Because of them, WiX continues to be the best deployment tool in the market.

About the Reviewers

Jiří Činčura is an independent .NET developer who focuses on data access layers and business layers as well as language constructs and databases. He is a project lead for ADO. NET, provider for the Firebird project, and Entity Framework support maintainer for the NuoDB database. He also creates custom large applications for various customers in Europe as well as companies from other countries. He conducts trainings and consultations about new technologies to provide customers the best information possible, to deliver applications in a shorter time and with better maintainability. When he's not programming or teaching, he spends time participating in ultra races.

Chris Eelmaa is a software engineer from Estonia, who has experience with a lot of different languages and technologies, some of which include C#, C++, WPF, WiX, and AngularJS. He works as a freelancer and contractor, interested in getting involved with projects that involve WPF and MVVM.

He is very keen on solving challenging problems and likes to understand exactly how or why something works; this has kept him in the engineering industry for over 8 years.

In his spare time, he likes to read about self-growth and meet similar people who aspire to grow. Chris also blogs at `http://chriseelmaa.com`.

Ranjith Sundarrajan is a father of a lovely daughter, Rachna, and a lucky husband to Vidya, a technologist at heart and an information scavenger. In his spare time, he enjoys asking "why" questions and finding an answer for them, and listening to different genres of music.

In the technology world, he is currently a technology expert at Tesco. He joined Tesco (www.tesco.com) as a developer in 2008 with a bachelor's degree from St. Joseph's College, Bangalore, and a master's degree in computer applications from BMS College, Bangalore.

He preaches writing quality code in the team and works extensively on .Net Compact Framework technologies, MS SQL Server, CI/CD, and TIBCO.

Being detail-oriented and data-driven, Ranjith is very passionate about technology and highly committed to providing quality solutions and products.

www.PacktPub.com

Support files, eBooks, discount offers, and more

For support files and downloads related to your book, please visit www.PacktPub.com.

Did you know that Packt offers eBook versions of every book published, with PDF and ePub files available? You can upgrade to the eBook version at www.PacktPub.com and as a print book customer, you are entitled to a discount on the eBook copy. Get in touch with us at service@packtpub.com for more details.

At www.PacktPub.com, you can also read a collection of free technical articles, sign up for a range of free newsletters and receive exclusive discounts and offers on Packt books and eBooks.

https://www2.packtpub.com/books/subscription/packtlib

Do you need instant solutions to your IT questions? PacktLib is Packt's online digital book library. Here, you can search, access, and read Packt's entire library of books.

Why Subscribe?

- Fully searchable across every book published by Packt
- Copy and paste, print, and bookmark content
- On demand and accessible via a web browser

Free Access for Packt account holders

If you have an account with Packt at www.PacktPub.com, you can use this to access PacktLib today and view 9 entirely free books. Simply use your login credentials for immediate access.

Table of Contents

Preface

The race to get software developed and deployed is reaching a dizzying pace. As companies accelerate their target release dates, topics such as continuous deployment, process automation, and DevOps take center stage. The need for a reliable and reproducible method of installing software is clear.

In this regard, it's easy to see where a tool like WiX can shine. Its XML syntax makes it easy to read, edit, and store in source control. It creates a package that can either be installed by nontechnical consumers with the click of a mouse or by a remote system administrator who needs to work from the command line. Probably its greatest strength is that it takes tasks that used to be performed by human beings and makes them automated. Think about installing databases, creating websites, and editing configuration files. These are all jobs that WiX can do at the time of installation. More than that, it can react to its environment, installing one file or another depending on the operating system, pulling down missing resources from the Web, and preventing installation on unsupported machines.

In this book, we'll cover many of these sorts of topics. Each chapter centers on a common theme, but taken together, they'll provide a good general overview of WiX's capabilities. You'll quickly see ways in which WiX can cut down on the time you might spend to manually set up your software now. For those who have only limited experience with WiX, the first few chapters should give you the background you need to be up and running. Those seeking to streamline their deployment processes will find the chapters on Windows user and group creation, file permissions, websites, and databases interesting. It's an exciting but challenging time for installation, and I hope you'll find that the recipes presented here give you the running start you'll need.

What this book covers

Chapter 1, Organizing and Building WiX Projects, helps you to build your WiX projects right, whether that means from Visual Studio, the command line, or on a build server with automation. We'll also see how to reference the output of other projects that will be included in the installer and how to separate WiX markup into libraries.

Chapter 2, Installing Files and Directories, covers creating folders and files on the end user's computer. We'll also see how to get heat.exe to generate this sort of markup for us and how to make decisions during installation about which files to create.

Chapter 3, File and Folder Permissions, introduces recipes to set the permissions on installed files and folders. We'll also see how to create file shares and choose a default program to use when opening a custom file type.

Chapter 4, Shortcuts, digs into all things related to shortcuts. We'll see how to put an icon on a shortcut, point a shortcut to a folder, as well as place a shortcut in the most popular places: the Start menu and the desktop. We'll also touch on how to create an advertised shortcut that will give users the ability to install features on demand.

Chapter 5, Editing XML Files during Installation, will come in handy especially when altering XML-based configuration files for your software. We'll add XML elements, remove them, set attributes, and insert inner text as part of our installation.

Chapter 6, Custom Actions, focuses on making well-behaved custom actions to extend the WiX functionality. We'll see how to protect the privacy of data sent to custom actions and open console windows without showing them, and rollback failures.

Chapter 7, Installing Wizards, puts a face on our installer by plugging in one of the wizards that comes with the WiX toolset. We'll then see how to customize it with our own images, license, and dialogs.

Chapter 8, Users and Groups, discusses adding users and groups to the target computer. We'll also see how to marry the two by adding users to groups and grant users the log on as a service security setting.

Chapter 9, Handling Prerequisites, includes tactics to only install our software to systems that can support it. We'll examine ways to stop an installation if prerequisites aren't met, install .NET Framework if it's missing, and download resources from the web during installation.

Chapter 10, Installing Websites, explores adding sites to IIS. We'll cover application pools, websites, virtual directories, and web applications. We'll then top it off with a recipe to secure a website with SSL.

Chapter 11, Linking to the Web, connects our installer to online resources. We'll see how to open web pages, display hyperlinks, and install shortcuts to websites.

Chapter 12, Installing SQL Server Databases, is dedicated to recipes about deploying SQL Server databases. If SQL Server isn't already installed on the target computer, we can install it with a bootstrapper. We'll add tables, insert data, and register an ODBC data source.

Chapter 13, Admin Tasks, rounds up a collection of administrative chores, including installing scheduled tasks, adding event sources, registering performance counters, and adding exceptions to the Windows firewall.

What you need for this book

To practice the recipes in this book, you will need the following:

- ▶ Visual Studio 2010 or newer (not the Express version)
- ▶ The WiX toolset, which can be downloaded from `http://wixtoolset.org`

Who this book is for

Developers who are already familiar with WiX will have the easiest time, but those with less experience will likely be able to follow along as well. If you are completely new to WiX and Windows Installer, then I recommend beginning with *WiX 3.6: A Developer's Guide to Windows Installer XML, Nick Ramirez, Packt Publishing*. It provides more context for the newcomer and walks the reader through the basics of setting up an installer. Here, we'll head off the beaten track and cover some topics relevant to more advanced scenarios.

Conventions

In this book, you will find a number of styles of text that distinguish between different kinds of information. Here are some examples of these styles, and an explanation of their meaning.

Code words in text, database table names, folder names, filenames, file extensions, pathnames, dummy URLs, and user input are shown as follows: "Behind the scenes, WiX introduces a new project type that has a `.wixproj` file extension."

A block of code is set as follows:

```
<ComponentGroup Id="SampleComponentGroup"
                Directory="SampleComponentsDirectory">
  <Component Id="cmpSampleTextFileTXT"
             Guid="{5382BC02-4484-4C9B-8734-A99D20632EA9}">
    <File Source="SampleTextFile.txt" />
  </Component>
</ComponentGroup>
```

When we wish to draw your attention to a particular part of a code block, the relevant lines or items are set in bold:

```
<ComponentGroup Id="SampleComponentGroup"
                Directory="SampleComponentsDirectory">
  <Component Id="cmpSampleTextFileTXT"
             Guid="{5382BC02-4484-4C9B-8734-A99D20632EA9}">
    <File Source="SampleTextFile.txt" />
  </Component>
</ComponentGroup>
```

Any command-line input or output is written as follows:

```
# msiexec /i InstallPackageA.msi /l*v install.log
```

New terms and **important words** are shown in bold. Words that you see on the screen, in menus or dialog boxes for example, appear in the text like this: "Select the **Setup Project** template from the list of available project types."

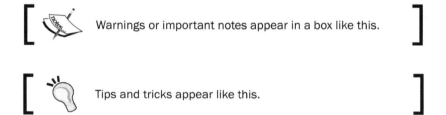

> Warnings or important notes appear in a box like this.

> Tips and tricks appear like this.

Reader feedback

Feedback from our readers is always welcome. Let us know what you think about this book—what you liked or may have disliked. Reader feedback is important for us to develop titles that you really get the most out of.

To send us general feedback, simply send an e-mail to feedback@packtpub.com, and mention the book title via the subject of your message.

If there is a topic that you have expertise in and you are interested in either writing or contributing to a book, see our author guide on www.packtpub.com/authors.

Customer support

Now that you are the proud owner of a Packt book, we have a number of things to help you to get the most from your purchase.

Downloading the example code

You can download the example code files for all Packt books you have purchased from your account at `http://www.packtpub.com`. If you purchased this book elsewhere, you can visit `http://www.packtpub.com/support` and register to have the files e-mailed directly to you.

Errata

Although we have taken every care to ensure the accuracy of our content, mistakes do happen. If you find a mistake in one of our books—maybe a mistake in the text or the code—we would be grateful if you would report this to us. By doing so, you can save other readers from frustration and help us improve subsequent versions of this book. If you find any errata, please report them by visiting `http://www.packtpub.com/submit-errata`, selecting your book, clicking on the **errata submission form** link, and entering the details of your errata. Once your errata are verified, your submission will be accepted and the errata will be uploaded on our website, or added to any list of existing errata, under the Errata section of that title. Any existing errata can be viewed by selecting your title from `http://www.packtpub.com/support`.

Piracy

Piracy of copyright material on the Internet is an ongoing problem across all media. At Packt, we take the protection of our copyright and licenses very seriously. If you come across any illegal copies of our works, in any form, on the Internet, please provide us with the location address or website name immediately so that we can pursue a remedy.

Please contact us at `copyright@packtpub.com` with a link to the suspected pirated material.

We appreciate your help in protecting our authors, and our ability to bring you valuable content.

Questions

You can contact us at `questions@packtpub.com` if you are having a problem with any aspect of the book, and we will do our best to address it.

1

Organizing and Building WiX Projects

In this chapter, we will cover the following topics:

- ▸ Installing WiX and creating a new project in Visual Studio 2013
- ▸ Referencing the output of a .NET console application in a WiX project by using a preprocessor variable
- ▸ Separating a portion of WiX markup into its own library
- ▸ Compiling a WiX installer on a build machine using MSBuild
- ▸ Building a WiX installer from the command line

Introduction

The trouble with any bit of code is handling the logistics of getting it from development to production. How do we work on it in our favorite IDE initially and then allow it to be built elsewhere? Perhaps on a build server that doesn't have access to the IDE?

WiX solves this problem for its own code by allowing it to be built using a variety of workflows. As part of the WiX toolset, we get the compiler and linker needed to create an MSI installer. If we're using Visual Studio then we also get project templates that use these tools on our behalf so that the entire build process is effortless. If we're trying to fit WiX into an automated deployment pipeline, we can either call the compiler and linker from the command line or use ready-made MSBuild tasks.

The recipes in this chapter are designed to get you comfortable when working with a WiX project in Visual Studio and also building it in various ways outside of the IDE. This way, you'll know how to get it from development to production with ease.

Installing WiX and creating a new project in Visual Studio 2013

It's possible to work with WiX outside of Visual Studio, but within it, you'll benefit from the project templates; IntelliSense and shortcuts to the compiler and linker settings are available on the project's properties. The only downside is that WiX doesn't work with Visual Studio Express. However, its installer will give you the compiler and linker so that you can still get work done even if you're using Notepad to write the markup. SharpDevelop, a free and open source IDE, also supports WiX projects.

Getting WiX up and running starts with downloading and running its installer. This is a one-stop shop to update Visual Studio, getting the compiler and linker as well as other utilities to work with MSI packages. WiX supports Visual Studio 2005 and later, including Visual Studio 2013, which we'll cover here. In this recipe, we will download and install WiX and create our first setup project.

Getting ready

To prepare for this recipe, install Visual Studio 2013 and close it before installing WiX.

How to do it...

Download and install the WiX toolset to get access to new project templates, IntelliSense, and project properties in Visual Studio. The following steps will guide you:

1. Open a browser, navigate to `http://www.wixtoolset.org`, and follow the link to the downloads page:

WiX Toolset v3.9

Rating: ⭐ ⭐ ⭐ ⭐ ⭐ Based on 1 rating	Released: Oct 31, 2014
Reviewed: 1 review	Updated: Oct 31, 2014 by robmen
Downloads: 15791	Dev status: Stable ❓

RECOMMENDED DOWNLOAD

wix39.exe

application, 20327K, uploaded Oct 30 - 13887 downloads

2. Once downloaded, launch the WiX installer and click on **Install**:

3. After completing the installation, open Visual Studio and go to **File** | **New** | **Project** | **Windows Installer XML**.

4. Select the **Setup Project** template from the list of available project types. The version of .NET that's displayed has no bearing on the project since it's comprised of XML mark-up and not .NET code. Give the project a name and click on **OK**:

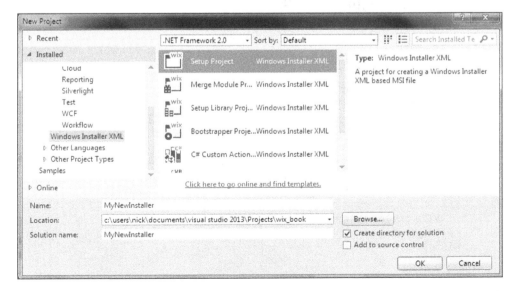

5. The project will initially include a file named `Product.wxs`, which contains the skeleton markup you'll need to create an installer:

```xml
<?xml version="1.0" encoding="UTF-8"?>
<Wix xmlns="http://schemas.microsoft.com/wix/2006/wi">
  <Product Id="*"
      Name="My Software"
      Language="1033"
      Version="1.0.0.0"
      Manufacturer="My Company"
      UpgradeCode="889e2707-5235-4d97-b178-cf0cb55d8ab8">
    <Package InstallerVersion="200"
      Compressed="yes"
      InstallScope="perMachine" />

    <MajorUpgrade DowngradeErrorMessage="A newer version of
[ProductName] is already installed." />
    <MediaTemplate />

    <Feature Id="ProductFeature"
      Title="MyFirstWixProject" Level="1">
      <ComponentGroupRef Id="ProductComponents" />
    </Feature>
  </Product>

  <Fragment>
    <Directory Id="TARGETDIR" Name="SourceDir">
      <Directory Id="ProgramFilesFolder">
        <Directory Id="INSTALLFOLDER"
          Name="My Software" />
      </Directory>
    </Directory>
  </Fragment>

  <Fragment>
    <ComponentGroup Id="ProductComponents"
      Directory="INSTALLFOLDER">
      <!-- TODO: Remove the comments around this Component
        element and the ComponentRef below in order to add
        resources to this installer. -->
      <!-- <Component Id="ProductComponent"> -->
        <!-- TODO: Insert files, registry keys, and other
          resources here. -->
      <!-- </Component> -->
    </ComponentGroup>
  </Fragment>
</Wix>
```

How it works...

The WiX team has always worked quickly to keep up with the latest versions of Visual Studio. For example, WiX 3.9 supports Visual Studio 2013. When we launched the installer, it checked which versions of Visual Studio were present and registered its project templates with all that were compatible.

Behind the scenes, WiX introduces a new project type that has a `.wixproj` file extension. This project file contains MSBuild markup, which points to the WiX compiler and linker. Other IDEs, such as SharpDevelop, can take advantage of these project files to build MSI packages too.

The `Product.wxs` file contains everything we need to get started with writing WiX markup. The best coding practices for how to structure a WiX file have been defaulted for you. For example, the `Directory` elements are separated into a `Fragment` element so that directories are decoupled from the files that will go into them. A `ComponentGroup` has been set up with a comment guiding you to add `Component` elements to it. Each version of WiX brings a better `Product.wxs` file with it.

There's more...

If you were curious about what effect changing the version of the .NET framework listed in the drop-down list at the top of the **New Project** window would have, the answer, at least for setup projects, is nothing at all. A WiX file contains XML and is compiled with a specialized WiX compiler, so the version of .NET that we select will ultimately be ignored. That's not to say that it doesn't make a difference for any of the other project types. For example, **C# Custom Action Project** will have a dependency on the version of .NET that's selected. Anyone who uses the installer that in turn uses that custom action will need to have that version of .NET installed.

Referencing the output of a .NET console application in a WiX project by using a preprocessor variable

After setting up our WiX project, the first thing we'll probably want to do is package up the files that we plan to install. Since we're working in Visual Studio, we'll likely want to include the output of other projects such as the `.exe` file that's created from a console application project. At first, we could try hardcoding the path to the file:

```
<Component Id="cmpMyConsoleAppEXE"
   Guid="{882DB6AA-1363-4724-8C43-2950E7ABECD4}">
   <File Source="..\MyConsoleApp\bin\Debug\MyConsoleApp.exe" />
</Component>
```

Although this works, it's a bit brittle and will break if the path to the file changes. Instead, we can use a preprocessor variable to store the path and allow Visual Studio to keep it up-to-date through the power of project references. In this recipe, we'll reference a console application's output and use a preprocessor variable to include that output in our installer.

Getting ready

To prepare for this recipe, create a new WiX setup project and name it `ConsoleAppInstaller`.

How to do it...

Use a preprocessor variable to get the path to a project's output with the following steps:

1. Add a new C# console application to the same solution as the `ConsoleAppInstaller` setup project by right-clicking on the solution in **Solution Explorer**, going to **Add | New Project... | Visual C# | Console Application** and naming it `TestApplication`. The name matters as we'll be referencing it later:

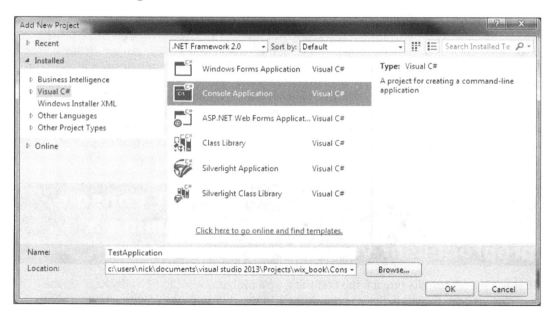

2. Within the setup project, add a reference to `TestApplication` by right-clicking on the **References** node in **Solution Explorer**, choosing **Add Reference...**, and finding `TestApplication` under the **Projects** tab. Click on **Add** and then on **OK**:

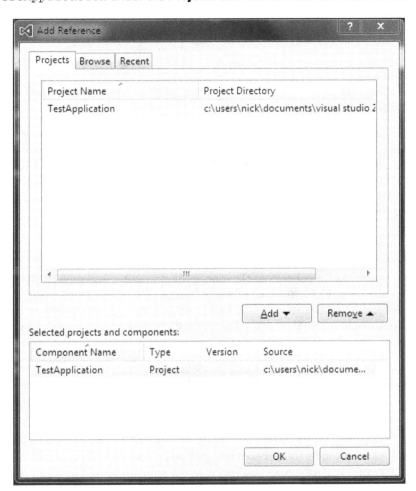

3. Within the setup project, open `Product.wxs` and replace the `ComponentGroup` markup inside the last fragment with the following code:

```
<ComponentGroup Id="ProductComponents"
  Directory="INSTALLFOLDER">
  <Component Id="cmpTestApplicationEXE"
    Guid="{6E2A6370-4784-4CF3-B42B-AA2D29EA5B1B}">
    <File Source="$(var.TestApplication.TargetDir)TestApplication.
exe" />
  </Component>
</ComponentGroup>
```

4. Build the project and `TestApplication.exe` will be included in the MSI file. Note that you must set the `EmbedCab` attribute on the `MediaTemplate` element to `yes` to include the CAB file that WiX creates, which is where our `.exe` file is stored, inside the MSI. Also, this example assumes that `TestApplication.exe` is the only file you'd like to include in the installer. Other files, such as DLLs, can be included in the same way though.

How it works...

When we referenced the C# console application within the WiX setup project, the preprocessor variable `$(var.[ProjectName].TargetDir)` was made available to us, where `ProjectName` in this case is `TestApplication`. `TargetDir` points to the output directory of the console application project where our compiled `TestApplication.exe` file can be found.

Other preprocessor variables are also made available. For example, `$(var.[ProjectName].TargetFileName)` gives you the name of the compiled application, which for us would be `TestApplication.exe`. A full list of these variables can be found at `http://wixtoolset.org/documentation/manual/v3/votive/votive_project_references.html`.

Another benefit of referencing the console application project in this way is that it ensures it is compiled before our setup project is. This way, our installer always includes the most up-to-date version of the application.

The GUID used for the `Guid` attribute on the `Component` element in this example can be any GUID, not just the one listed. You can generate a new one in Visual Studio by navigating to **Tools | Create GUID**. Use **Registry Format** as the GUID's format. More information can be found at `http://wixtoolset.org/documentation/manual/v3/howtos/general/generate_guids.html`.

You can also set the `Guid` attribute to an asterisk (*) or omit it altogether and WiX will set the GUID for you. You should choose your own if you plan on authoring a patch file for the application in the future or if the contents of `Component` don't contain an element that can be marked as a `KeyPath` element.

Separating a portion of WIX markup into its own library

As a project grows in complexity and size, we may end up with different teams building different parts of the software in relative isolation. Each team may want to control how their module will be installed or, during development, install only the modules that their code depends upon into their dev environment. To handle these scenarios, we can split our installer into chunks of WiX code called setup libraries.

A setup library can be compiled independently and plugged into the main, monolithic setup project later. We can also include the library in a team-owned setup project that only contains the modules required by the team. In essence, we can mix and match libraries wherever we need them to create installers for different purposes.

You might also want to share some complex installer markup, such as a user interface, with other installers, and a library is the perfect way to do this. Although it's outside the scope of this book, setup libraries are also used when building custom WiX extensions. In this recipe, we'll see how to create a setup library and include it in our setup project.

Getting ready

To prepare for this recipe, create a setup project and call it `SetupLibraryInstaller`.

How to do it...

Add a setup library to the solution and reference it in a setup project. The following steps show how to do this:

1. Add a new setup library to the same solution as the setup project by right-clicking on the solution in **Solution Explorer** and navigating to **Add | New Project... | Windows Installer XML | Setup Library Project**. For this example, name the project MySetupLibrary:

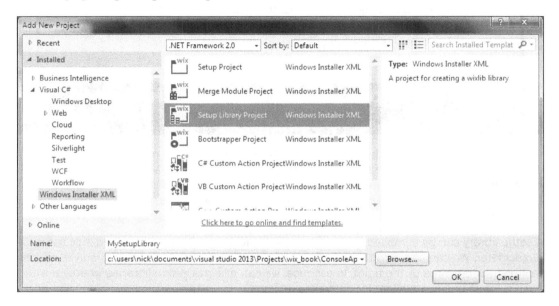

2. After it's created, right-click on the MySetupLibrary project in **Solution Explorer** and go to **Add | New Item... | Text File**. Name the text file SampleTextFile.txt and click on **Add**. Our library will install this single text file.

3. Right-click on the MySetupLibrary project in **Solution Explorer** again and select **Properties**. Select the **Tool Settings** tab and add -bf, which stands for bind files, to the librarian textbox, as shown in the following screenshot:

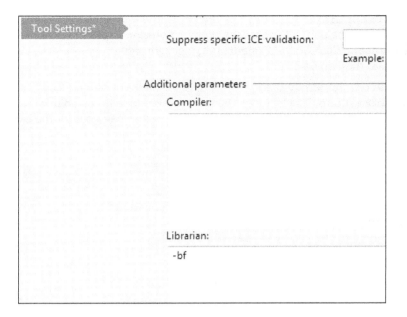

4. Open `Library.wxs` and replace the existing markup with the following:

```xml
<?xml version="1.0" encoding="UTF-8"?>
<Wix xmlns="http://schemas.microsoft.com/wix/2006/wi">
  <Fragment>
    <DirectoryRef Id="INSTALLFOLDER">
      <Directory Id="SampleComponentsDirectory"
        Name="Sample Components" />
    </DirectoryRef>

    <ComponentGroup Id="SampleComponentGroup"
      Directory="SampleComponentsDirectory">
      <Component Id="cmpSampleTextFileTXT"
        Guid="{5382BC02-4484-4C9B-8734-A99D20632EA9}">
        <File Source="SampleTextFile.txt" />
      </Component>
    </ComponentGroup>

    <Feature Id="SampleFeature">
      <ComponentGroupRef Id="SampleComponentGroup" />
    </Feature>
  </Fragment>
</Wix>
```

5. In the `SetupLibraryInstaller` project, add a reference to the setup library by right-clicking on the **References** node in **Solution Explorer** and selecting **Add Reference....** Click on the **Projects** tab, highlight `MySetupLibrary`, click on **Add**, and then on **OK**.

6. Open `Product.wxs` and add a `FeatureRef` element with an ID of `SampleFeature`. This includes the feature we added to the `Library.wxs` file of `SetupLibrary` in our installer. `FeatureRef` can go after the existing `Feature` element as follows:

```
<Feature Id="ProductFeature"
         Title="ConsoleAppInstaller"
         Level="1">
  <ComponentGroupRef Id="ProductComponents" />
</Feature>
<FeatureRef Id="SampleFeature"/>
```

How it works...

Our setup library contains WiX markup to install a single text file called `SampleTextFile.txt`. Ordinarily, when you build a library like this, the source files don't get stored within it. Instead, only the WiX markup is compiled without any of the source files it refers to. In that case, we would have had to copy `SampleTextFile.txt` to the setup project's directory too, so that it can be found at link-time when compiling the installer.

However, because we added the `-bf` flag, which stands for bind files, to the Librarian settings, the text file was serialized and stored within the library. The `-bf` flag will handle serializing and storing any type of file including executables, images, and other binary data. Setup libraries are compiled into files with a `.wixlib` extension.

The markup we added to the library created a component, directory, and feature for the text file. To integrate the new directory with the existing directory structure as defined by our setup project, we chose to reference `INSTALLFOLDER` with a `DirectoryRef` element. Just be sure that there's a corresponding `Directory` element in your setup project that has this name. At link time, the `DirectoryRef` element in the library is merged with the `Directory` element in the setup project by matching their IDs. Once we had this, we were able to add a new subdirectory within the `INSTALLFOLDER` directory called **Sample Components**. After installation, we can see that the new directory was created and it contains our text file:

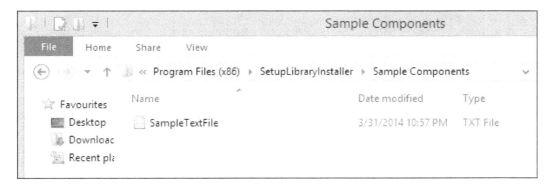

To be sure that our library gets compiled before our setup project, we referenced it within the setup project using the **References** node. Then, to create a link to the library, we included a `FeatureRef` element in `Product.wxs`, which had an ID matching the `Feature` defined in the library. This pulls the `Feature` with all of its components into the installer.

There's more...

The setup libraries might contain more than just components, features, and directories. For example, they might define markup for a user interface using a `UI` element, which could then be linked to our installer with a `UIRef` element. Basically, if you can find a corresponding `*Ref` element, such as `DirectoryRef`, `UIRef`, `ComponentGroupRef`, or `FeatureRef`, then you'll be able to separate that type of element into a library and use its `*Ref` element to link it to the setup project.

Even if you can't find a corresponding `*Ref` element, as long as you have a reference of some kind, such as `Property` and `PropertyRef`, the rest of the elements in the library will be carried along with it into the installer. So, at the very least, you could include a single `Property` in the library and use that as the link between the library elements and the installer.

Compiling a WiX installer on a build machine using MSBuild

The WiX Toolset places its compiler and linker in `C:\Program Files (x86)\WiX Toolset v3.9\bin`. This is fine when compiling on your own machine but becomes a concern when you'd like to share your project with others or have it compile on a build server. WiX will have to be installed on each computer that builds the project.

Alternatively, we can store the WiX tools in source control, and then whoever needs to build a setup project can get everything they need by cloning the repository. This will also help us keep a handle on which version of WiX we're compiling against on a project-by-project basis.

In this recipe, we'll store the WiX binaries in a fictitious source control directory on the `C:` drive. We'll then update the `.wixproj` file of a setup project to use the MSBuild tasks stored there. I will be using a server with the Windows Server 2012 R2 operating system installed on it. You should be able to follow along with other versions of Windows Server.

Getting ready

To prepare for this recipe, perform the following steps:

1. Install the .NET Framework 3.5. It's needed by the WiX build tasks. In Windows Server 2012 R2, it can be installed as a feature within **Server Manager**:

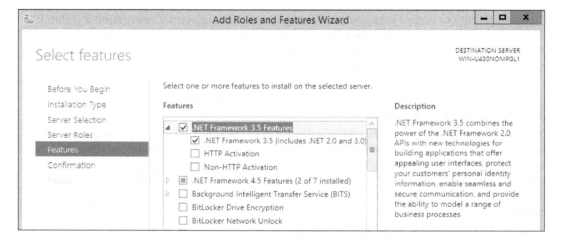

2. Next, we'll need the MSBuild engine, which is part of Microsoft Build Tools. It can be downloaded from `http://www.microsoft.com/en-us/download/details.aspx?id=40760`.

3. After installing MSBuild, add its installation directory to the computer's `PATH` environment variable. Get there by right-clicking on **This PC** in file explorer and then going to **Properties | Advanced system settings | Environment Variables...**. Scroll through the list of system variables until you find the one labeled `Path`. Highlight it, click on **Edit...**, and then add the path to the MSBuild directory into the **Variable value** field, preceded by a semicolon. Then, click on **OK**:

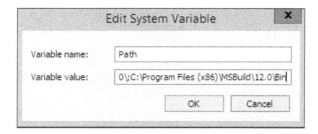

How to do it...

Download the WiX binaries and update your setup project to use the included MSBuild tasks:

1. Open a browser, navigate to `http://www.wixtoolset.org`, and follow the link to the downloads page. Download `wix39-binaries.zip`:

2. Make sure that the ZIP file is unblocked by right-clicking on it, choosing **Properties**, clicking on **Unblock** (if you don't see it, just continue to the next step), and then on **OK**.

3. Extract the contents of the ZIP file to `C:\SourceControl\WiX39`. Perform this step on both the server and on your own development computer so that our WiX projects can be built in both places using the MSBuild tasks from this folder (note that in a real-world scenario, our source control system would be responsible for copying the binaries to each computer):

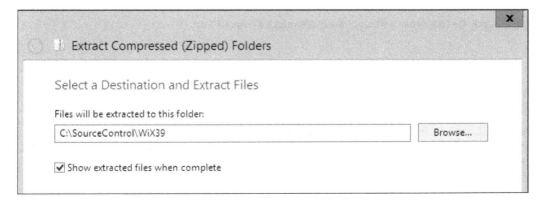

4. We will build a simple setup project to confirm that we've got everything on the server configured correctly. Create a setup project on your development machine and call it `BuildMachineInstaller`.

5. Open the `BuildMachineInstaller.wixproj` file and add the `WixToolPath`, `WixTargetsPath`, and `WixTasksPath` properties as shown, making sure that the value of `WixToolPath` ends in a backslash:

```
<PropertyGroup>
    <Configuration Condition=" '$(Configuration)' == '' ">Debug</
Configuration>
    <Platform Condition=" '$(Platform)' == '' ">x86</Platform>
    <ProductVersion>3.9</ProductVersion>
    <ProjectGuid>f80ca9fc-8e42-406e-92f9-06e484e94d67</
ProjectGuid>
    <SchemaVersion>2.0</SchemaVersion>
    <OutputName>BuildMachineInstaller</OutputName>
    <OutputType>Package</OutputType>
    <WixToolPath>C:\SourceControl\WiX39\</WixToolPath>
    <WixTargetsPath>$(WixToolPath)wix.targets</WixTargetsPath>
    <WixTasksPath>$(WixToolPath)WixTasks.dll</WixTasksPath>
    <WixTargetsPath Condition=" '$(WixTargetsPath)' == '' AND
'$(MSBuildExtensionsPath32)' != '' ">$(MSBuildExtensionsPath32)\
Microsoft\WiX\v3.x\Wix.targets</WixTargetsPath>
    <WixTargetsPath Condition=" '$(WixTargetsPath)' == ''
">$(MSBuildExtensionsPath)\Microsoft\WiX\v3.x\Wix.targets</
WixTargetsPath>
</PropertyGroup>
```

6. Copy the `BuildMachineInstaller` solution folder and all of its subfolders to `C:\SourceControl` on the build server.

7. Open a command prompt via **Run | cmd**, execute the following commands to change the directory to the `BuildMachineInstaller` folder and compile the solution using MSBuild:

```
cd C:\SourceControl\BuildMachineInstaller

msbuild BuildMachineInstaller.sln
```

How it works...

We started with a blank slate of a freshly installed Windows Server 2012 R2 operating system. Therefore, we had to install all the required software including .NET Framework 3.5 and Microsoft Build Tools 2013. The latter gives us the MSBuild engine, whose path we included in the computer's PATH environment variable.

Next, we downloaded the WiX binaries and copied them to `C:\SourceControl`. With a source control system, these files could be shared among all computers that need to compile our setup projects. We also had to update our project's `.wixproj` file so that it knew where to find these WiX binaries. This is accomplished by adding three MSBuild properties: `WixToolPath`, `WixTargetsPath`, and `WixTasksPath`. The first property sets the path to the WiX binaries, the second to the `wix.targets` file, and the third to `WixTasks.dll`. With all of this setup out of the way, we opened a command prompt, navigated to the folder where our solution file was on the build server, and compiled it using MSBuild.

Building a WiX installer from the command line

WiX has excellent integration with Visual Studio, but that shouldn't stop you from using it in other IDEs. We ought to be able to create an installer using only Notepad and the WiX compiler and linker if we wanted to. Luckily, WiX gives us the freedom to do this. In this recipe, we'll write a simple `.wxs` file and compile it into an MSI package using Candle, which is the WiX compiler, and Light, which is the WiX linker.

Getting ready

To prepare for this recipe, perform the following steps:

1. Using a text editor such as Notepad, create a file called `Product.wxs` and add the following markup to it:

```xml
<?xml version="1.0" encoding="UTF-8"?>
<Wix xmlns="http://schemas.microsoft.com/wix/2006/wi">
  <Product Id="*"
           Name="My Software"
           Language="1033"
           Manufacturer="My Company"
           Version="1.0.0.0"
           UpgradeCode="8c7d85db-b0d1-4a9a-85ea-130836aeef67">

    <Package InstallerVersion="200"
             Compressed="yes"
             InstallScope="perMachine" />

    <MajorUpgrade DowngradeErrorMessage="A newer version of
[ProductName] is already installed." />
    <MediaTemplate EmbedCab="yes" />

    <Feature Id="ProductFeature"
             Title="The main feature"
             Level="1">
      <ComponentGroupRef Id="ProductComponents" />
```

```
      </Feature>
   </Product>

   <Fragment>
     <Directory Id="TARGETDIR" Name="SourceDir">
       <Directory Id="ProgramFilesFolder">
         <Directory Id="INSTALLFOLDER"
                           Name="My Software" />
       </Directory>
     </Directory>
   </Fragment>

   <Fragment>
     <ComponentGroup Id="ProductComponents"
                         Directory="INSTALLFOLDER">
       <Component Id="cmpMyTextFileTXT"
                     Guid="{A4540658-09B6-46DA-8880-0B1962E06642}">
         <File Source="MyTextFile.txt" />
       </Component>
     </ComponentGroup>
   </Fragment>
</Wix>
```

2. This installs a text file called `MyTextFile.txt`. So, add a text file with this name to the same directory as `Product.wxs`. We will compile the two files from the command line to create an installer.

How to do it...

Open a command prompt and use `candle.exe` and `light.exe` to compile and link our WiX source file:

1. Open a command prompt by navigating to **Run | cmd**.

2. Change the directory to where the `Product.wxs` and `MyTextFile.txt` files are using the following command line:

   cd C:\MyProject

3. Use Candle to compile the `.wxs` file into a `.wixobj` file and then place it in an output folder called `obj`. Be sure to surround the path to Candle, `%WIX%bin\candle`, with quotes since it will contain spaces when it is expanded:

   "%WIX%bin\candle" *.wxs -o obj

4. Use Light to link the text file and the `.wixobj` file together to form an MSI:

   "%WIX%bin\light" obj*.wixobj -o bin\CommandLineInstaller.msi

How it works...

When we installed the WiX toolset, it gave us the WiX compiler, which is `candle.exe`, and linker, which is `light.exe`. These are the only tools we need to create an MSI from our WiX source file, `Product.wxs`. From the command line, we navigated to the directory where our source file was and then used Candle and Light to compile and link the file to create an MSI installer.

The first argument we passed to Candle was `*.wxs`. This selects all the `.wxs` files in the current directory and includes them in the compilation. Next, the `-o` argument tells Candle where to send the output of the compilation step. In this case, we sent it to a directory called `obj`. Note that the directory name ends in a backslash so that Candle knows that it's a directory. If it didn't exist before, it will be created.

The output of the Candle command was a file called `Product.wixobj`. This was an intermediate file that was picked up by `light.exe` in the next step. The first argument we passed to Light was the location of the `.wixobj` files: `obj\*.wixobj`. By using an asterisk, we select all the `.wixobj` files in the `obj` directory. The `-o` argument tells Light where to create the MSI file and what to name it. In this case, we create a file called `CommandLineInstaller.msi`.

Name	Date modified	Type
CommandLineInstaller.msi	11/20/2014 11:05 ...	Windows Installer ...
CommandLineInstaller.wixpdb	11/20/2014 11:05 ...	WIXPDB File

Another file called `CommandLineInstaller.wixpdb` was also created. This can be used when building patch files. You can learn more by reading Peter Marcu's blog post *WiX: Introducing the WixPdb* at `http://petermarcu.blogspot.com/2008/02/wix-introducing-wixpdb.html`.

There are a number of arguments that can be passed to Candle and Light that you might want to get to know. Passing the `-?` flag to either will give you a list of all the available options:

```
"%WIX%bin\candle" -?
```

```
"%WIX%bin\light" -?
```

We used the `%WIX%` system environment variable to resolve the path to the WiX bin directory, where `candle.exe` and `light.exe` are present. This variable is added when you install the WiX toolset and resolves to `C:\Program Files (x86)\WiX Toolset v3.9`. It will not be present if you are using the WiX binaries directly without installing the WiX toolset.

2

Installing Files and Directories

In this chapter, we will cover the following recipes:

- ▶ Installing directories onto the target computer
- ▶ Adding a file to a directory
- ▶ Installing a 64-bit executable file to Program Files
- ▶ Including one component or another depending on the condition
- ▶ Using the `heat.exe` tool to generate components

Introduction

The WiX team has chosen to use XML as its modus operandi. It's a good thing that they have, because the declarative syntax of XML lends itself well to changing the state of the end user's computer without being tied to the details of how it was done. If they had chosen a procedural language instead, such as C, then we would be obliged to write functions to perform installation tasks. Other installers, such as NSIS, take the procedural route.

The problem with a procedural approach is that it's implementation-specific. If working with a Windows XP filesystem is different than working with a Windows 10 filesystem, then we will need to have branching logic to call a different function depending on where our installer runs. XML lets us declare what we want the state of the system to look like and Windows Installer takes care of the details of making it happen. Truth be told, the Windows Installer platform is itself declarative. Behind the scenes, it creates tables of relational data that declare the changes to make to the target system.

XML has another benefit, especially with regards to creating directories and files. It's great for representing a hierarchy. We can easily nest the `Directory` elements inside of other `Directory` elements to create subdirectories. Similarly, we can nest the `File` elements inside the `Directory` elements to add files to a specific directory. In this chapter, we'll get some practice creating directories, files, and components. We'll also see how useful the `Heat` utility is, since it can create all of this markup for us.

Installing directories onto the target computer

Before we can install any files to the end user's system, we have to specify the directories where they'll go. These could be directories that already exist or new ones that we'll be creating. Either way, we'll be using the `Directory` elements to form our folder structure. Our `Directory` elements can be nested directly within our `Product` element or separated into a `Fragment`. The `Fragment` approach has the advantage of being more modular, or in other words, keeps the concerns of making a directory structure separate from other chores such as installing files into those directories.

In this recipe, we will install some directories into the `Program Files` folder. To keep things simple, we won't install any files yet. Since Windows Installer won't install empty directories, we'll have to put some kind of placeholder in for now. We can use the `CreateFolder` element for this. Its job is simply to ensure the directory gets created even though it's empty.

Getting ready

To prepare for this recipe, create a new setup project and call it `DirectoryInstaller`.

How to do it...

Define a `Directory` element that targets the `Program Files` folder and then nest subdirectories within it. The following steps show you how it is done:

1. The default markup that we find in our `Product.wxs` file already contains the skeleton of a directory structure. A `Directory` with an `ID` of `ProgramFilesFolder` targets `Program Files`:

```
<Fragment>
  <Directory Id="TARGETDIR" Name="SourceDir">
    <Directory Id="ProgramFilesFolder">
      <Directory Id="INSTALLFOLDER"
                 Name="DirectoryInstaller" />
    </Directory>
  </Directory>
</Fragment>
```

Downloading the example code

You can download the example code files for all Packt Publishing books you have purchased from your account at http://www.packtpub.com. If you purchased this book elsewhere, you can visit http://www.packtpub.com/support and register to have the files e-mailed directly to you.

2. Remove the directory that has an ID of INSTALLFOLDER, replacing it with the following where each Directory element's ID is unique and the name is the friendly name of the folder. This will create three folders—Config, Tools, and Documentation—within a folder called My Software that's within a folder called My Company:

```
<Directory Id="ProgramFilesFolder">
  <Directory Id="MyCompanyFolder" Name="My Company">
    <Directory Id="MySoftwareFolder" Name="My Software">
      <Directory Id="ConfigFolder" Name="Config" />
      <Directory Id="ToolsFolder" Name="Tools" />
      <Directory Id="DocFolder" Name="Documentation" />
    </Directory>
  </Directory>
</Directory>
```

3. To ensure our empty directories are created, update the ComponentGroup that's at the bottom of the default Product.wxs file with the following Component elements. Each contains the CreateFolder tag that will allow its directory to be installed:

```
<Fragment>
  <ComponentGroup Id="ProductComponents">
    <Component Id="cmpCreateConfigFolder"
               Guid="{21AC0239-87F9-4D8B-9F73-71665C491150}"
               Directory="ConfigFolder">
      <CreateFolder />
    </Component>
    <Component Id="cmpCreateToolsFolder"
               Guid="{7B75B591-58B7-41F4-A511-E221E243371C}"
               Directory="ToolsFolder">
      <CreateFolder />
    </Component>
    <Component Id="cmpCreateDocFolder"
               Guid="{B0BA1D63-110C-4169-9094-64F4103234E8}"
               Directory="DocFolder">
      <CreateFolder />
    </Component>
  </ComponentGroup>
</Fragment>
```

How it works...

The first thing to notice is that the top-level `Directory` element has the ID `TARGETDIR` and the name of `SourceDir`:

```
<Directory Id="TARGETDIR" Name="SourceDir">
```

This is how all directory structures should begin and is required by Windows Installer. `TARGETDIR` identifies the hard drive where our installation will go and, by default, is set to the largest drive on the system. That's usually the `C:` drive but even if it isn't, the child `Directory` element with the ID `ProgramFilesFolder` leaves no doubt where the files should go. From there, we can add subdirectories of our own. If you'd like to begin your directory structure under a different existing folder, see the following link for information about other built-in `Directory` elements: `http://msdn.microsoft.com/en-us/library/aa370905(v=vs.85).aspx#system_folder_properties`. Note that predefined directories such as `ProgramFilesFolder` don't get a `Name` attribute.

For new directories that you create, the ID can be anything as long as it follows a few rules:

- It must be unique among other `Directory` elements
- It should contain only letters, numbers, underscores, and periods
- It must begin with either a letter or an underscore

Windows Installer uses this identifier internally, but the end user will never see it. The `Name` attribute, on the other hand, sets the visible name of the folder after it's installed. After installation, we can see that the directory structure was added to the computer under `Program Files`:

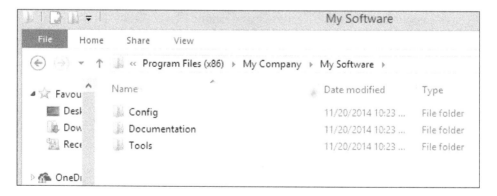

Adding a file to a directory

Markup to copy files to the end user's computer is probably going to make up the bulk of your installer. That's because for each file you want to install, which may number in the hundreds, there will be a corresponding XML element in your .wxs file to represent it. In this recipe, we'll cover the basics—installing a single text file to a directory that we'll create under Program Files. All file-types, whether plain text or binary, will follow this same pattern.

Getting ready

To prepare for this recipe, perform the following steps:

1. Create a setup project and call it FileInstaller.

2. Add a text file to the project and name it Sample.txt. Although we're adding the file directly to the setup project, in most cases the source files we use will be from other projects or folders.

3. Update the default directory structure to the following wherein a folder called My Software is added to the Program Files directory:

```
<Fragment>
  <Directory Id="TARGETDIR" Name="SourceDir">
    <Directory Id="ProgramFilesFolder">
      <Directory Id="INSTALLFOLDER" Name="My Software" />
    </Directory>
  </Directory>
</Fragment>
```

How to do it...

Use ComponentGroup to install a collection of files to a directory as shown in the following steps:

1. By default, Product.wxs already contains a ComponentGroup that has a Directory attribute set to INSTALLFOLDER. This is exactly the syntax we want and will install any child Component elements to the My Software folder:

```
<Fragment>
  <ComponentGroup Id="ProductComponents"
                  Directory="INSTALLFOLDER">
  </ComponentGroup>
</Fragment>
```

2. Add a `Component` element to the `ComponentGroup` with an `Id` of your choosing and generate a new GUID for the `Guid` attribute:

```
<ComponentGroup Id="ProductComponents"
                Directory="INSTALLFOLDER">
  <Component Id="cmpSampleTXT"
             Guid="{759CE9A8-F4DF-4DE7-B995-E5F0D926BE43}">
  </Component>
</ComponentGroup>
```

3. Within that component, add a `File` element that points to our `Sample.txt` file:

```
<Component Id="cmpSampleTXT"
           Guid="{759CE9A8-F4DF-4DE7-B995-E5F0D926BE43}">
  <File Source="Sample.txt" />
</Component>
```

4. Although the setup project template already sets it up for you, make sure that the `Id` of the `ComponentGroup` is referenced by a `ComponentGroupRef` element inside of a `Feature` element:

```
<Feature Id="ProductFeature" Title="The Software" Level="1">
  <ComponentGroupRef Id="ProductComponents" />
</Feature>
```

How it works...

`ComponentGroup` is a container for a group of `Component` elements. It's really handy when declaring where the components should be installed to since it comes with a `Directory` attribute for specifying this. Any child `Component` elements will go into that directory on the target computer. It points to the `Id` of a `Directory` element.

Each component is in turn a container for a single `File` element and, through the use of its GUID, allows the file to be tracked from version to version. For example, if we need to patch the file in the future, we'll be able to match it by this identifier. The GUID uniquely identifies it among all other components that have been installed to the end user's system. The ID is used to differentiate the component within the MSI package. You can use any identifier you like, but as a convention, I prefix mine with `cmp`.

The `File` element points to our source file on disk with its `Source` attribute. In this example, we used the relative path `Sample.txt`, but we could have used an absolute path or a preprocessor variable. Note that we added the text file directly to our setup project, but in practice the files you reference do not need to be in the project. As long as the path to the file is correct, the `WiX` linker will find it.

There's more...

If all the files in the ComponentGroup can be found in the same directory on your development computer then you can save yourself some typing by setting the ComponentGroup element's Source attribute. In the following example, we use the Source attribute to specify that all child components can be found in the SourceFiles directory. For this to work, you must switch all File elements in the group to use the Name attribute, rather than the Source attribute, to specify the name of the file. The code is as follows:

```
<ComponentGroup Id="ProductComponents"
                Directory="INSTALLFOLDER"
                Source="..\SourceFiles">
  <Component Id="cmpSampleTXT"
             Guid="{759CE9A8-F4DF-4DE7-B995-E5F0D926BE43}">
    <File Name="Sample.txt" />
  </Component>
</ComponentGroup>
```

Installing a 64-bit executable file to Program Files

The 64-bit revolution has come and gone. If you're still writing 32-bit applications, you should make the switch if you can. Modern Windows operating systems have full support for it, but for end users to see the benefits, the software needs to be updated to take advantage. The 64-bit programs have the potential for increased performance, better parallel processing, and improved security. See the Technet article at http://technet.microsoft.com/en-us/library/dd630755%28v=office.12%29.aspx for more information.

Once the decision has been made to convert software to 64 bits, the next step is ensuring it's installed to the correct Program Files folder and that our installer identifies itself as being compatible with the 64-bit architecture. In this recipe, we will build a console application that targets the x64 platform and then include it in an MSI package that supports it.

Getting ready

To prepare for this recipe, perform the following steps:

1. Create a new setup project and call it `SixtyFourBitInstaller`.

2. Within the same solution, add a C# console application project and name it `ConsoleApp64Bits`. Make sure that it targets .NET 4 or later, since we'll need it for the utility method that checks whether we're running in a 64-bit process. To ensure it will run in a 64-bit process on a 64-bit machine, make sure that **Platform target** on the **Build*** tab of the project's properties is set to either **x64** or **Any CPU**:

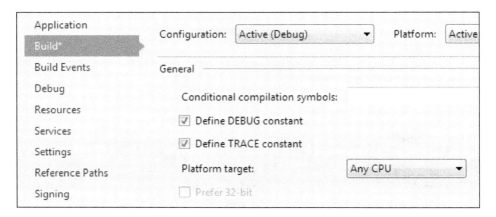

3. Update the application's `Program.cs` file with the following code:

```
using System;

namespace ConsoleApp64Bits
{
  class Program
  {
    static void Main(string[] args)
    {
      if (Environment.Is64BitProcess)
      {
        Console.WriteLine("Process is 64-bits!");
      }
      else
      {
        Console.WriteLine("Process is NOT 64-bits!");
      }
```

```
        Console.ReadKey();
    }
  }
}
```

4. Add a reference to the console application in our setup project by right-clicking on the **References** node in **Solution Explorer** and going to **Add Reference...** | **Projects** | **ConsoleApp64Bits** | **Add** | **OK**.

How to do it...

Set the `-arch` flag to `x64` and then set your files to install to the 64-bit program files:

1. Right-click on the setup project in **Solution Explorer** and go to **Properties** | **Tool Settings**. Then, in the **Compiler** textbox, add `-arch x64`:

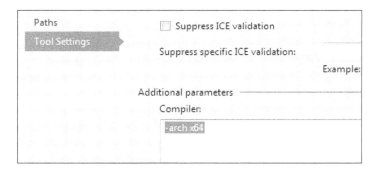

2. Replace the existing directory structure in `Product.wxs` with the following code, making sure to use `ProgramFiles64Folder` instead of `ProgramFilesFolder`:

```
<Fragment>
  <Directory Id="TARGETDIR" Name="SourceDir">
    <Directory Id="ProgramFiles64Folder">
      <Directory Id="INSTALLFOLDER" Name="My Software" />
    </Directory>
  </Directory>
```

3. Add a `Component` and `File` element for the 64-bit console application, as shown in the following code:

```
<Fragment>
  <ComponentGroup Id="ProductComponents"
                  Directory="INSTALLFOLDER">
    <Component Id="cmpConsoleApp64BitsEXE"
               Guid="{7230A6C1-2920-43A0-B9BA-69E4B0A5450C}">
```

```
        <File Source="$(var.ConsoleApp64Bits.TargetDir)
ConsoleApp64Bits.exe" />
      </Component>
    </ComponentGroup>
  </Fragment>
```

4. Run the installer and then check that `ConsoleApp64Bits.exe` was installed in `C:\ Program Files\My Software`. Run the application and see that it's running in a 64-bit process.

How it works...

An installer has some metadata in it that tells what platform it's targeting, or more accurately, what platform the files it's installing are targeting. In this example, we are packaging up a 64-bit console application. Therefore, the installer should convey that. That's where the `-arch` flag comes in. By setting it to **x64** in the **Compiler** settings, we're setting up that metadata.

On 64-bit Windows, there are two program files folders: `Program Files` for 64-bit software and `Program Files (x86)` for 32-bit software. In our setup project, we swapped the directory that, by default, has `Id` of `ProgramFilesFolder` with one that has `Id` of `ProgramFiles64Folder`. As the name implies, this will reference the 64-bit `Program Files` folder.

The next step was to install our application to this directory. The `ComponentGroup` element has a `Directory` attribute to specify which directory to install its child components to. We set it to `INSTALLFOLDER` and since that folder is a subdirectory of `ProgramFiles64Folder`, we can be sure that it will install to the 64-bit `Program Files`.

There's more...

It's possible to include 32-bit executable files in your 64-bit installer and have them installed to `Program Files (x86)`. First, be sure that you've added the `Directory` elements for both `ProgramFilesFolder` and `ProgramFiles64Folder`:

```
<Directory Id="ProgramFilesFolder">
  <Directory Id=" INSTALLFOLDER_X86" Name="My Software" />
</Directory>
<Directory Id="ProgramFiles64Folder">
  <Directory Id="INSTALLFOLDER" Name="My Software" />
</Directory>
```

Then, for those components that are meant to be installed to `Program Files (x86)`, set the `Win64` attribute on the `Component` element to `no`. This alerts the installer that this particular file is not 64-bits.

Here's an example that installs a 32-bit executable to `Program Files (x86)`:

```
<ComponentGroup Id="My32BitComponents"
                Directory="INSTALLFOLDER_X86">
  <Component Id="cmpConsoleApp32BitsEXE"
             Guid="{61F4DDB4-07B9-475C-BE34-07BA619DA86F}"
             Win64="no">
    <File Source="$(var.ConsoleApp32Bits.TargetDir)ConsoleApp32Bits.
exe" />
  </Component>
</ComponentGroup>
```

We store the 32-bit component in its own `ComponentGroup` that's separate from our other components. Then, we can use the `Directory` attribute to install child components to `INSTALLFOLDER_X86`.

Including one component or another depending on the condition

An installer should be able to adapt to its surroundings, to mold itself to the operating system or other constraints it detects. WiX has this sort of intelligence baked in. By using conditions, we can prevent a component from being installed if it's not a good fit and simultaneously allow a different component to be installed.

In this recipe, we'll store two XML files in the MSI and select only one of them to install based on the target operating system. We'll be using a built-in property called `VersionNT` to get the operating system, but this can be extended by defining our own custom properties. For example, you might install a component if the user selects `Yes` for a radio button in the user interface. Or, you might install debug versions of your DLLs depending on whether you're installing to a development machine.

Getting ready

To prepare for this recipe, perform the following steps:

1. Create a setup project and name it `ConditionalComponentsInstaller`.
2. Add an XML file to the project and call it `Windows7.xml`.
3. Add a second XML file and call it `Windows8.xml`.

How to do it...

Add a `Condition` element to `Component` to install it only if the condition is `true`, such as if the version of Windows matches our expectation:

1. Add a `Component` for each XML file:

```
<ComponentGroup Id="ProductComponents"
                Directory="INSTALLFOLDER">
  <Component Id="cmpWindows7XML"
             Guid="{1FDA4A47-B45B-4040-A486-56EDA4B036B8}">
    <File Source="Windows7.xml" />
  </Component>
  <Component Id="cmpWindows8XML"
             Guid="{2FF087CE-9483-4456-BF77-FB1F6D700A76}">
    <File Source="Windows8.xml" />
  </Component>
</ComponentGroup>
```

2. Add the `Condition` elements inside each component. Use the predefined `VersionNT` property to check the version of Windows that's installed. For Windows 7, the value of this property will be automatically set to `601`. For Windows 8, it will be `602`:

```
<Component Id="cmpWindows7XML"
           Guid="{1FDA4A47-B45B-4040-A486-56EDA4B036B8}">
  <File Source="Windows7.xml" />
  <Condition>VersionNT = 601</Condition>
</Component>
<Component Id="cmpWindows8XML"
           Guid="{2FF087CE-9483-4456-BF77-FB1F6D700A76}">
  <File Source="Windows8.xml" />
  <Condition>VersionNT = 602</Condition>
</Component>
```

How it works...

In this recipe, we're installing two XML files. However, the first will only be installed if the operating system is Windows 7 and the second only if it's Windows 8. We started by adding components in the way that we always have. The trick was to add the `Condition` elements to each, comparing a property called `VersionNT` to a number that represents a version of Windows.

The `VersionNT` property is built into Windows Installer without you having to set it. Each version of Windows gets a number that we can compare with this property to see which operating system we're dealing with. Specific values for `VersionNT` can be found on Microsoft's MSDN website at `http://msdn.microsoft.com/en-us/library/aa370556(v=vs.85).aspx`. You might not find Windows 8.1 in the list, since it's so new, but its value is `603`. Other built-in properties can be found at `http://msdn.microsoft.com/en-us/library/aa370905(v=vs.85).aspx`.

We used an equals sign (=) to do a comparison:

```
<Condition>VersionNT = 601</Condition>
```

We could have checked for any operating system greater than Windows 7 by using the greater-than-or-equal-to operator (>=), such as:

```
<Condition>VersionNT >= 601</Condition>
```

Similarly, we could have checked whether the operating system was Windows 7 or older by using the less-than-or-equal-to operator (<=):

```
<Condition><![CDATA[VersionNT <= 601]]></Condition>
```

In this case, we had to surround the statement with the `CDATA` tags so that our less-than sign wouldn't be confused with the surrounding XML. We can also combine two expressions to see if the operating system falls within a range, such as Windows 7 through Windows 8.1 inclusive:

```
<Condition>
  <![CDATA[VersionNT >= 601 AND VersionNT <= 603]]>
</Condition>
```

There's more...

The `Component` element has an attribute called `Transitive` that, when set to `yes`, will cause any `Condition` within the `Component` to be re-evaluated if the installer is rerun, as shown in the following code:

```
<Component Id="cmpWindows7XML"
           Guid="{1FDA4A47-B45B-4040-A486-56EDA4B036B8}"
           Transitive="yes">
```

Here, if the child `Condition` evaluates to false the second time around, the component will be removed from the end user's computer. Alternatively, if the condition evaluates to true, the component will be installed even if it hadn't been before.

Using the heat.exe tool to generate components

Sometimes, your software is going to require a lot of files: there's the main executable, supporting libraries, images, configuration files, help documentation, and potentially more. You might start out writing the `Component` elements by hand, but pretty soon it's going to amount to more than you'd care to take on.

The WiX team has provided a tool called Heat to shoulder the burden. You can take this utility and point it at a directory of files, and it will generate the WiX markup for you. In this recipe, we'll try it out by creating a directory of text files and then run Heat to turn it into a `.wxs` file. Heat is included in the WiX toolset.

Getting ready

To prepare for this recipe, perform the following steps:

1. On your desktop, create a folder named `SourceFiles`.
2. Add three text files to it and name them `Sample1.txt`, `Sample2.txt`, and `Sample3.txt`.

How to do it...

Call `heat.exe` from the command line to convert a folder of files into the WiX markup using the following steps:

1. Open a command prompt and change the directory to your `Desktop` folder:

   ```
   cd Desktop
   ```

2. Invoke `heat.exe` on the folder with the following command:

   ```
   "%WIX%bin\heat.exe" dir "SourceFiles" -cg MyComponentGroup
   -dr INSTALLFOLDER -gg -sfrag -srd -var var.SourceFilesDir -out
   "Components.wxs"
   ```

3. Check that a file called `Components.wxs` was created on your desktop. Create a new WiX setup project and copy the `Components.wxs` file into it. You can do this by dragging the file onto the Visual Studio Solution Explorer.

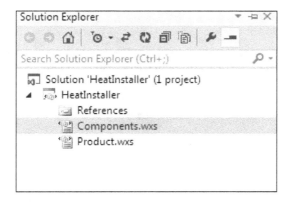

4. Define a preprocessor variable called `SourceFilesDir` as the path to the `Desktop\SourceFiles` folder by opening your setup project's properties and selecting the **Build** tab. Then, add `SourceFilesDir=C:\Users\Nick\Desktop\SourceFiles` to the textbox that's labeled **Define preprocessor variables**. You can also use a relative path. Use the path to your own Desktop.

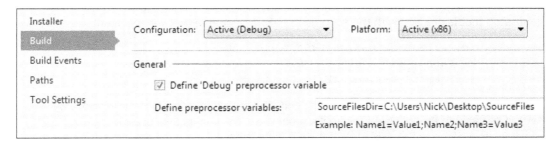

5. To reference our new components in the project, add a `ComponentGroupRef` element to our project's `Product.wxs` file. Its ID should match the ID of `ComponentGroup` that Heat generated for us in the `Components.wxs` file:

```
<Feature Id="ProductFeature" Title="HeatInstaller" Level="1">
  <ComponentGroupRef Id="ProductComponents" />
  <ComponentGroupRef Id="MyComponentGroup"/>
</Feature>
```

How it works...

Our call to Heat began with the `dir` harvest type. The term `harvest` means to generate WiX markup from a source. There are several things that can be harvested, including Visual Studio projects, single standalone files and, in this case, a whole directory; hence, the `dir` harvest type is used. Immediately following the harvest type is the directory where the source files can be found. In this case, we named the folder `SourceFiles`.

The `-cg` flag instructs `heat.exe` to create a `ComponentGroup` element and the `Id` to assign to it; in this case, we used `MyComponentGroup`. All the components that Heat generates will be included in this group.

Next, we set the `-dr` flag to `INSTALLFOLDER` so that our components can be installed to that directory. The `-gg` flag generates GUIDs for the components. The `-sfrag` flag causes all the components to be put into a single `Fragment` tag, rather than having each in its own `Fragment` tag. The `-srd` flag tells Heat to not create a `Directory` element with the name `SourceFiles`, which it would have done otherwise.

The `-var` flag causes each `File` element to have a `Source` attribute prefixed with a preprocessor variable of our choice. Here's an example of a `File` element that would be generated that is prefixed with the `SourceFilesDir` variable that we specified:

```
<File Id="filB6C392508320F3B45A8928D279282132"
      KeyPath="yes"
      Source="$(var.SourceFilesDir)\Sample2.txt" />
```

Having this variable in place allows us to specify the path to our text files dynamically by setting its value in the WiX setup project's properties. The last flag we used was `-out`, which gives a name to the `.wxs` file that Heat generates.

We copied the `Components.wxs` file to a setup project and defined the `SourceFilesDir` preprocessor variable so that it pointed to the folder on our desktop. The reason that we need to do this is that the `.wxs` file only contains markup to add the files. The actual source files themselves must still be linked-in during compilation. Finally, we added a `ComponentGroupRef` element within our `Feature` so that the new components would be included in the MSI.

There's more...

In this recipe, we did all of our work from the command line. We can do the same job within a setup project's `.wixproj` file using the MSBuild syntax. That way, the latest files will be pulled in each time we build the project. The key is to use the `HeatDirectory` task.

Here's an example where we've added a `HeatDirectory` task inside of the `BeforeBuild` target in our `.wixproj` file:

```
<Target Name="BeforeBuild">
  <PropertyGroup>
    <WixToolPath>C:\Program Files (x86)\WiX Toolset  v3.8\bin\</WixToolPath>
  </PropertyGroup>
  <HeatDirectory ToolPath="$(WixToolPath)"
                 Directory="$(ProjectDir)SourceFiles"
                 ComponentGroupName="MyComponentGroup"
                 DirectoryRefId="INSTALLFOLDER"
                 GenerateGuidsNow="true"
                 SuppressFragments="true"
                 SuppressRootDirectory="true"
                 PreprocessorVariable="var.SourceFilesDir"
                 OutputFile="Components.wxs" />
</Target>
```

As before, the `SourceFilesDir` preprocessor variable would need to be defined in the project's properties and `MyComponentGroup` should be added as `ComponentGroupRef` within the feature. Also, we will need to add the `Component.wxs` file to the project after the first time that it's generated. From then on, it will be automatically updated for you each time you build the project.

If you're using a version control system such as TFS that locks your files between checkouts, you may not want to check-in the `Components.wxs` file itself, since it will constantly change.

More information about the `HeatDirectory` task can be found at `http://wixtoolset.org/documentation/manual/v3/msbuild/task_reference/heatdirectory.html`.

3
File and Folder Permissions

In this chapter, we will cover the following recipes:

- ▶ Changing the permissions on a folder for a user
- ▶ Changing the permissions on a file for a user
- ▶ Marking a file as read only
- ▶ Creating a file share
- ▶ Setting the default program for a file type

Introduction

When it comes to security, your first line of defense is limiting the number of users who are authorized to access or modify your software's files and folders. In Windows, **access control lists** (**ACL**) enumerate the permissions each user has. A user in the list can either be granted a permission directly or inherit it by being a member of a Windows group. For example, being a member of the **Administrators** group gives full control to read, execute, and modify a file or the contents of a folder.

In this chapter, we will see how to set the ACLs of files and folders. We'll then talk about some other tricks that WiX has to offer, such as how to convert a regular folder into a file share and how to assign the default program to be used when opening a type of file.

Changing the permissions on a folder for a user

When you set permissions on a folder, all of the files that are created within that folder after that point will inherit those permissions. This accommodates the Windows Installer's sequence, which as luck would have it, creates folders first and then adds files to them. This means we can set permissions once and let them trickle down. In this recipe, we'll give a user named Joe full access to a folder.

Getting ready

To prepare for this recipe, perform the following steps:

1. Create a new setup project and name it `FolderPermissionsInstaller`.

2. Add a text file named `Sample.txt` to the project. After installation, we can verify that the permissions that were set on the folder propagated to this file. Add a `Component` element to include it in the installation:

```
<ComponentGroup Id="ProductComponents"
                Directory="INSTALLFOLDER">
  <Component Id="cmpSampleTXT"
             Guid="{79972677-2109-471C-A8FE-58A255CE43E3}">
    <File Source="Sample.txt" />
  </Component>
</ComponentGroup>
```

3. The user for whom we are setting permissions must already exist. Manually, create a user named `Joe` on the target computer by right-clicking on **This PC** and going to **Manage | Local Users and Groups**. Right-click on the **Users** node and select **New User**. Set the user's name as `Joe` as shown here:

How to do it...

Place `util:PermissionEx` inside a `CreateFolder` element to set permissions on a folder. The following steps will show you how to do it:

1. Reference `UtilExtension` by right-clicking on the **References** node in **Solution Explorer**, going to **Add Reference...** | **Browse**, and then adding `WixUtilExtension.dll`.

2. Add the `UtilExtension` namespace to the `Wix` element in `Product.wxs`:

   ```
   <Wix xmlns="http://schemas.microsoft.com/wix/2006/wi"
   xmlns:util="http://schemas.microsoft.com/wix/UtilExtension">
   ```

3. Within the `ComponentGroup` that's set to be installed to our installation directory, add a `Component` that has a child element `CreateFolder`:

```
<ComponentGroup Id="ProductComponents"
                Directory="INSTALLFOLDER">
  <Component Id="cmpEmptyFolder"
             Guid="{292A233A-9C0E-479F-B83B-509F841B32D3}">
    <CreateFolder>
    </CreateFolder>
  </Component>
</ComponentGroup>
```

4. Add a `util:PermissionEx` element inside the `CreateFolder` element and set the name of the user we're giving access to, and the type of permissions to allow. The following code grants full access to the folder and the files it contains:

```
<CreateFolder>
  <util:PermissionEx User="Joe" GenericAll="yes" />
</CreateFolder>
```

How it works...

The `PermissionEx` element is stored in an assembly called `WixUtilExtension.dll` that we must reference before we can use it. To make things easy, the **Add Reference...** window takes us directly to the WiX `bin` folder where that file can be found. The second step is to add the `UtilExtension` XML namespace to our `Product.wxs` file. To do so, we added `xmlns:util` followed by the `UtilExtension` namespace, `http://schemas.microsoft.com/wix/UtilExtension`, to our `Wix` element. Afterwards, any element from `WixUtilExtension.dll` can be accessed by prefixing it with `util`.

By placing `PermissionEx` inside a `CreateFolder` element, which in turn is inside a `Component` element, we're instructing WiX to update the permissions on the directory that the component is being installed to. We can also use the `CreateFolder` element's `Directory` attribute to identify a directory to set permissions on. In that case, the folder that the component is being installed to doesn't matter.

The first attribute that we added to `PermissionEx`, `User`, identifies the user that our installer will grant folder permissions to. This user must either already exist on the target computer or be created by the installer. Otherwise, the installation will fail.

The second attribute, `GenericAll`, gives the user read, write, and execute permissions on the folder. Alternatively, we can specify each one individually with the `GenericRead`, `GenericWrite`, and `GenericExecute` attributes. More information about the `PermissionEx` element can be found at `http://wixtoolset.org/documentation/manual/v3/xsd/util/permissionex.html` and information about how Windows treats the different permissions available on MSDN at `http://msdn.microsoft.com/en-us/library/bb727008.aspx`.

Although `GenericAll`, `GenericWrite`, and `GenericExecute` can be set alone, `GenericRead` can't be the only permission. You can, however, pair it with the `Read` attribute to give the user read-only access.

There's more...

There's another element, also called `PermissionEx`, that's included in the core WiX toolset and is not part of `UtilExtension`. It only has two attributes: `Id` and `Sddl`. It allows you to set the permissions on a file or folder using **Security Descriptor Definition Language** (**SDDL**). Because it's more complex and the UtilExtension's version of `PermissionEx` will suit most of your needs, I recommend that you only use this specialized element if your use case demands a more fine-tuned approach. It will only work where Windows Installer 5.0 is installed, which includes Windows 7 and newer operating systems.

There's also a `Permission` element in the core toolset that has many of the same attributes as `util:PermissionEx`. However, while `PermissionEx` will keep any existing ACLs on the folder, `Permission` wipes them all out and applies only those that you've explicitly set.

Changing the permissions on a file for a user

Although setting access at the folder level is good for quickly securing all of your files in one fell swoop, we can still fine-tune permissions on a file-by-file basis. This might be useful, for example, if you have a main executable that can be run by anyone but another administrative utility that should only be run by certain users.

In this recipe, we'll install a text file and update its permissions so that our user Joe has full access.

Getting ready

To prepare for this recipe, perform the following steps:

1. Create a new setup project and name it `FilePermissionsInstaller`.
2. Add a text file named `Sample.txt` to the project and then add a `Component` element to include it in the installation:

```
<ComponentGroup Id="ProductComponents"
                Directory="INSTALLFOLDER">
  <Component Id="cmpSampleTXT"
            Guid="{FB746118-B1E5-42DC-AA76-862C4E1EABCF}">
    <File Source="Sample.txt">
    </File>
  </Component>
</ComponentGroup>
```

3. The user for whom we are setting permissions must already exist. Manually, create a user named `Joe` on the target computer by right-clicking on **This PC** and going to **Manage | Local Users and Groups**. Right-click on the **Users** node and select **New User**. Set the user's name as `Joe`.

How to do it...

As shown in the following steps, include `util:PermissionEx` inside a `File` element to set permissions on a file:

1. Reference `UtilExtension` by right-clicking on the **References** node in **Solution Explorer**, going to **Add Reference... | Browse**, and then adding `WixUtilExtension.dll`.

2. Add the `UtilExtension` namespace to the `Wix` element in `Product.wxs`:

```
<Wix xmlns="http://schemas.microsoft.com/wix/2006/wi"
xmlns:util="http://schemas.microsoft.com/wix/UtilExtension">
```

3. Find the `File` element that you want to set permissions on and then add a `util:PermissionEx` element inside it. Specify the user to whom you'd like to give access and the type of permissions to allow. The following code grants full access to the `Sample.txt` file for a user named `Joe`:

```
<File Source="Sample.txt">
    <util:PermissionEx User="Joe" GenericAll="yes"/>
</File>
```

How it works...

We began by adding a reference to `WixUtilExtension.dll` and including the `UtilExtension` namespace, `http://schemas.microsoft.com/wix/UtilExtension`, in the `Wix` element. This gives us access to the `PermissionEx` element.

By putting `PermissionEx` inside a `File` element, we're saying that we want to update the permissions on this particular file after we've installed it. The `User` attribute selects the user to give access to and the `GenericAll` attribute gives them read, write, and execute permissions. You can learn more about the other attributes that are available at `http://wixtoolset.org/documentation/manual/v3/xsd/util/permissionex.html`.

You can view the permissions on a file by opening its properties and selecting the **Security** tab:

Here, a user named Joe has been given full access to read, write, and modify the file.

Marking a file as read only

The primary reason for making a file *read only* is to prevent it from being accidentally modified. This could apply to end-user license agreements, readme files, and other documents that the user might open with a text editor such as Word.

In this recipe, we'll install a text file and then set its **Read-only** flag.

Getting ready

To prepare for this recipe, create a new setup project and name it ReadOnlyInstaller.

How to do it...

Set the `ReadOnly` attribute on a `File` element to prevent it from being accidentally modified with the following steps:

1. Add a `File` element within `Component` to install a file called `Sample.txt`:

```
<ComponentGroup Id="ProductComponents"
                Directory="INSTALLFOLDER">
  <Component Id="cmpSampleTXT"
             Guid="{44BB2441-F98C-41F9-A1FE-EB732B626CF4}">
    <File Source="Sample.txt" />
  </Component>
</ComponentGroup>
```

2. Add the ReadOnly attribute to the `File` element to mark that file as read only:

```
<File Source="Sample.txt" ReadOnly="yes" />
```

How it works...

The `File` element has an attribute called `ReadOnly` that when set to `yes`, marks that file as read only after it's been installed. You can see this setting on a file by opening its properties and looking at the `Attributes` section:

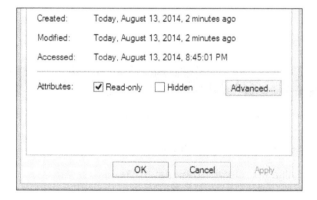

Creating a file share

Sometimes, an application needs to allow others on the network to access its files. For example, it may produce log files that should be available to anyone who wants to see them without having to first log onto the computer where the application is installed. By putting those files into a file share, others on the network can access them. In this recipe, we'll see how to convert a normal directory into a file share and set the permissions on it.

Getting ready

To prepare for this recipe, create a new setup project and call it `FileShareInstaller`.

How to do it...

To create a file share, use the `FileShare` element of `UtilExtension` and then configure its permissions with the `FileSharePermission` element:

1. Reference `UtilExtension` by right-clicking on the **References** node in **Solution Explorer**, going to **Add Reference...** | **Browse**, and then adding `WixUtilExtension.dll`.

2. Add the `UtilExtension` namespace to the `Wix` element in `Product.wxs`:

```
<Wix xmlns="http://schemas.microsoft.com/wix/2006/wi"
xmlns:util="http://schemas.microsoft.com/wix/UtilExtension">
```

3. Use the following `Directory` elements to add a folder called `Shared Folder` to the end user's computer:

```
<Directory Id="TARGETDIR" Name="SourceDir">
  <Directory Id="ProgramFilesFolder">
    <Directory Id="INSTALLFOLDER" Name="My Software">
      <Directory Id="FileShareDirectory"
                 Name="Shared Folder" />
    </Directory>
  </Directory>
</Directory>
```

4. Create a `ComponentGroup` that targets that directory:

```
<ComponentGroup Id="SharedFilesComponents"
                Directory="FileShareDirectory">
</ComponentGroup>
```

5. Within the `ComponentGroup`, add a component that contains a `util:FileShare` element. Be sure to mark `Component` with the `KeyPath` attribute:

```
<ComponentGroup ...>
  <Component Id="cmpFileShare"
             Guid="{6974184A-1F4F-4FBB-ADA6-826E9C947A7C}"
             KeyPath="yes">
    <util:FileShare Id="myFileShare"
                    Description="Shares some stuff"
                    Name="MyFileShare">
    </util:FileShare>
  </Component>
</ComponentGroup>
```

6. Within the same `Component` tag, add a `util:User` element that names an existing user to whom we will give access to the file share. You can use the `Everyone` user to grant access to everybody:

```
<Component ...>
  <util:FileShare ...>
  <util:User Id="everyoneUser"
             Name="Everyone"
             CreateUser="no"
             RemoveOnUninstall="no"/>
</Component>
```

7. Add a `util:FileSharePermission` element inside the `util:FileShare` element to give the user we just referenced access to the folder:

```
<util:FileShare ...>
  <util:FileSharePermission User="everyoneUser"
                            GenericAll="yes" />
</util:FileShare>
```

8. Add a ComponentGroupRef element within the existing Feature to reference our new ComponentGroup:

```
<Feature Id="ProductFeature" Title="FileShareInstaller" Level="1">
<ComponentGroupRef Id="ProductComponents" />
<ComponentGroupRef Id="SharedFilesComponents" />
</Feature>
```

How it works...

A directory is converted to a network file share by including the `FileShare` and `FileSharePermission` elements within it. These become available after referencing `WixUtilExtension.dll` and adding the `UtilExtension` namespace to our `Wix` element. We set up a hierarchy of `Directory` elements and chose one of them to become the file share, identifying it as `FileShareDirectory`.

The `FileShare` element is wrapped in a `Component` that's installed to the target directory. It takes the `Id`, `Description`, and `Name` attributes. The `Id` uniquely identifies the element within the MSI database. `Description` gives you a chance to explain about its contents and `Name` lets you label the file share, apart from the actual name of the folder as set by the `Directory` element. For example, the actual name of the folder is `Shared Folder`, but users on the network will access it through its share name, `\\ [PC_Name] \MyFileShare`.

It's required that we add a `FileSharePermission` element inside `FileShare` so that it can be accessed by at least one user. Just prior to adding it, we referenced an existing user called `Everyone` with a `User` element. Its `Name` attribute identifies the user to find. Since `Everyone` is a built-in account that should already exist on the computer, we set both `CreateUser` and `RemoveOnUninstall` to `no`. Using `Everyone` will allow anyone on the network to access the folder. If your use case requires tighter control over who should have access, you can select a different user—possibly one that you're creating as part of the installation.

With the `FileSharePermission` element, we granted the `Everyone` user full access to the folder by setting the `GenericAll` attribute to `yes`. It can be a little tricky figuring out which attributes on the `FileSharePermission` element to set to get the desired result. The following table sums up what you need to grant **Full control**, **Change**, and **Read** access:

Permission	FileSharePermission attributes
Full control	`GenericAll`
Change	`GenericWrite`, `GenericRead`, `Traverse`, and `Delete`
Read	`GenericRead` and `Traverse`

The file share permissions are different from the regular permissions on a folder. To see them, right-click on the folder and go to **Properties | Sharing | Advanced Sharing... | Permissions**.

When it comes to adding files to a file share, remember that it's just a normal directory that has been converted. You can add files in the normal way using the `File` and `Component` elements. Also, the share will be removed along with the rest of your application during an uninstall. Even if new files have been added to it, which would cause the directory itself to remain after uninstalling, it will no longer be registered as a file share.

Setting the default program for a file type

Maybe you're packaging up a media player that processes MP3 files, or perhaps it's photo editing software that must consume JPEG files. Many applications must interact with specialized file types, and occasionally companies develop proprietary data formats that are stored in files with custom extensions. For example, Photoshop files use the `.psd` file extension.

In this recipe, we'll see how to set the application that we're installing as the default program to use for a certain type of file. We'll use the extension `.xyz`. Our application will be opened when the end user double-clicks on a file called `test.xyz` that we'll create.

Getting ready

To prepare for this recipe, perform the following steps:

1. Create a setup project and name it `DefaultProgramInstaller`.

2. Our application will process `.xyz` files. So, within the same Visual Studio solution, add a C# Console Application project, name it `XyzHandler`, and replace the code in `Program.cs` with the following:

```
using System;
using System.IO;

namespace XyzHandler
{
  class Program
  {
    static void Main(string[] args)
    {
      if (args.Length == 0 || string.IsNullOrEmpty(args[0]))
      {
        Console.WriteLine("No file name given.");
      }
      else
      {
        string fileName = args[0];
        if (File.Exists(fileName))
        {
```

```
            Console.WriteLine(File.ReadAllText(fileName));
         }
         else
         {
            Console.WriteLine("File not found.");
         }
      }

      Console.WriteLine("Press any key to exit.");
      Console.ReadKey();
   }
  }
}
```

How to do it...

Use the `ProgId`, `Extension`, and `Verb` elements to set the default program to use for a type of file:

1. Within the setup project, add a reference to the `XyzHandler` project.

2. Install the `XyzHandler` application using a `Component` and `File` element:

```
<Component Id="cmpXyzHandlerEXE"
           Guid="{C7F9458A-BFBF-4BB5-8DEC-3FD859B9C6EF}">
  <File Id="xyzHandlerEXE"
        Source="$(var.XyzHandler.TargetDir)XyzHandler.exe" />
</Component>
```

3. Add another `Component` tag that will establish `XyzHandler.exe` as the default program for the `.xyz` files and set its `KeyPath` attribute to `yes`. Add a `ProgId` element inside it:

```
<Component Id="cmpXyzHandlerProgId"
           Guid="{1FA51F40-88BD-4C0C-8B07-B9BF200D338E}"
           KeyPath="yes">
  <ProgId Id="xyzFile"
          Description="XYZ Document">
  </ProgId>
</Component>
```

4. Add an `Extension` element inside the `ProgId`. Its `Id` attribute will identify the file type that our console application handles. Set its `ContentType` attribute to `text/plain`:

```
<ProgId ...>
  <Extension Id="xyz" ContentType="text/plain">
  </Extension>
</ProgId>
```

5. Inside the `Extension`, add a `Verb` element that will open our application and pass it the name of the file that the end user has double-clicked on:

```
<Extension ...>
  <Verb Id="open"
        TargetFile="xyzHandlerEXE"
        Argument="&quot;%1&quot;" />
</Extension>
```

6. After installation, open Notepad and write the following lines: You are processing an XYZ file. Save it as test.xyz. Be sure that the file truly is saved with a `.xyz` file extension and not as `test.xyz.txt`.

How it works...

First, we added a `Component` tag that includes `XyzHandler.exe` in our installer. We then added a `Component` tag that contained a `ProgId` element. The `ProgId` element creates an entry in the Windows registry on the end users' computer under `HKEY_LOCAL_MACHINE\SOFTWARE\Classes\.xyz`. This is what registers our application as the program to use when the end user double-clicks on a file that has the `.xyz` extension. Similarly, the value we set in the `Description` attribute will be stored in the registry under `HKEY_LOCAL_MACHINE\SOFTWARE\Classes\xyzFile`. We'll see this description when we hover our cursor over an `.xyz` file.

We then added an `Extension` element inside the `ProgId` element. This is where we identify the `.xyz` extension as the one that our application will handle. Since our `.xyz` file will really just be a text file in disguise, we used the `text/plain` content type, or, as it's more accurately called, media type. **Internet Assigned Numbers Authority (IANA)** maintains a list of all registered media types. It can be found at `http://www.iana.org/assignments/media-types/media-types.xhtml`. When an organization creates a new file extension, it will often register it with IANA.

The `Verb` element opens `XyzHandler.exe` for any `.xyz` file. Its `TargetFile` element references the `File` element in the `cmpXyzHandlerEXE` component. The `Argument` attribute sets the parameters to pass to `XyzHandler.exe`. In this case, we are passing the name of the clicked file, surrounded by double quotes.

If we have added a file called `test.xyz` that has `You are processing an XYZ file` written to it, then we should see our program launch when we double-click on it:

There's more...

If you'd like to associate a certain icon with the .xyz files, then add the Icon attribute to the ProgId element. It should point to a File element that references an .ico file. For example, after adding an .ico file to the project, we will add a new Component that references the icon, as follows:

```
<Component Id="cmpRocketICO"
           Guid="{3B136AF8-BB3F-4B75-AC1B-F633DD79CE92}">
  <File Id="rocketICO"
        Source="rocket.ico" />
</Component>
```

We can then reference that icon on ProgId via its Icon attribute:

```
<ProgId Id="xyzFile"
        Description="XYZ Document"
        Icon="rocketICO">
```

Now, any .xyz file will display the icon that we've installed:

Note that after uninstalling, it may take a computer restart before the icon is removed from the existing .xyz files.

4
Shortcuts

In this chapter, we will cover the following recipes:

- ▶ Adding an application shortcut to the **Start** menu
- ▶ Adding an icon to a shortcut
- ▶ Placing a shortcut on the desktop
- ▶ Creating a shortcut to a folder
- ▶ Creating an advertised shortcut that installs a feature on demand

Introduction

Shortcuts offer a big convenience for users, allowing them to launch applications and open directories without having to search through their C: drive to get to them. During installation, we can add shortcuts to the Windows **Start** menu, the user's desktop, or any other directory we choose. Shortcuts can be customized with icons and labels, and they can even specify command-line switches to pass to the target application.

We can also create a special type of shortcut, called an advertised shortcut that acts as a link to a feature that we haven't installed yet. When the user clicks on the shortcut for the first time, the feature will be installed on demand. In this chapter, we'll explore several types of shortcuts that are commonly used.

Adding an application shortcut to the Start menu

The Windows **Start** menu is probably the first place that a user will look for a shortcut. Things got a little interesting with Windows 8, in which the traditional **Start** menu was removed and Windows 8.1 in which it makes a return, but shows no application shortcuts. However, we can still see shortcuts in the **Apps** view, which you can get to by going to the new **Start** screen and clicking on the down arrow:

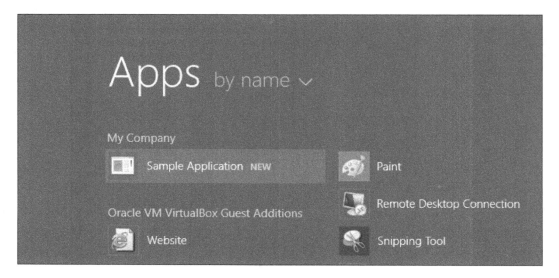

In short, remember to think about the version of Windows you're installing to when it comes to the **Start** menu shortcuts.

In this recipe, we will create a shortcut to our application that is displayed on the Windows **Start** menu. It will be installed for all users, meaning that any user that logs on will see it. It's also possible, as we'll discuss, to install a shortcut only for the current user.

Getting ready

To prepare for this recipe, perform the following steps:

1. Create a new setup project and call it `StartMenuShortcutInstaller`.
2. Add a **C# Console Application** project to the same Visual Studio solution and call it `SampleApplication`. Add the following code snippet to its `Program.cs` file:

```
using System;

namespace SampleApplication
```

```
{
  public class Program
  {
    public static void Main(string[] args)
    {
      Console.WriteLine("Running the sample application");

      if (args.Length > 0 && !string.IsNullOrEmpty(args[0]))
      {
        // Print command-line argument if given
        Console.WriteLine(args[0]);
      }

      Console.ReadKey();
    }
  }
}
```

3. Reference the console application project in the setup project.

4. Add a `Component` element to it so that it will be included in the installation:

```
<ComponentGroup Id="ProductComponents"
                Directory="INSTALLFOLDER">
  <Component Id="cmpSampleApplicationEXE"
             Guid="{478BC1B5-9429-4E7D-A045-E97E6DBB9EEC}">
    <File Source="$(var.SampleApplication.TargetDir)
SampleApplication.exe" />
  </Component>
</ComponentGroup>
```

How to do it...

Add a `Directory` element targeting `ProgramMenuFolder` and then add a Component with a `Shortcut` element to it. The following steps will show you how to do it:

1. Within your hierarchy of `Directory` elements, add one that has an `ID` of `ProgramMenuFolder`. Components installed here will be displayed on the Windows **Start** menu. The following snippet creates a subfolder in the `Start` menu called `My Company`:

```
<Directory Id="TARGETDIR" Name="SourceDir">
  <Directory Id="ProgramFilesFolder">
    <Directory Id="INSTALLFOLDER" Name="My Company" />
  </Directory>
  <Directory Id="ProgramMenuFolder">
```

```
        <Directory Id="MyCompanyStartMenuFolder"
          Name="My Company" />
      </Directory>
    </Directory>
```

2. Add a component with a `Shortcut` element in it. The `Shortcut` element's `Target` attribute identifies the file to be launched and its `Directory` attribute defines where to place the shortcut:

```
<ComponentGroup ...>
  <Component Id="cmpMyShortcut"
    Guid="{705722CC-89CC-451C-81CD-F0FA4453BC18}">
    <Shortcut Id="SampleApplicationShortcut"
        Name="Sample Application"
        Description="Runs the sample application"
        Directory="MyCompanyStartMenuFolder"
        Target="[INSTALLFOLDER]SampleApplication.exe" />
  </Component>
</ComponentGroup>
```

3. Within that same component, add a `RemoveFolder` element so that our **Start** menu's subfolder is removed during uninstallation. Also, add a `RegistryValue` element with a `KeyPath` attribute set to yes:

```
<Component ...>
  <Shortcut ... />
  <RemoveFolder Id="RemoveCompanyStartMenuFolder"
      Directory="MyCompanyStartMenuFolder"
      On="uninstall" />

  <RegistryValue Root="HKCU"
      Key="Software\My Company\Sample Application"
      Name="installed"
      Type="integer"
      Value="1"
      KeyPath="yes" />
</Component>
```

How it works...

In this example, we added a shortcut in the **Start** menu that will launch our simple console application, which we installed in the `Program Files` folder. Our directory structure probably already contains a `Directory` element for `ProgramFilesFolder`. We just need to add another `Directory` element for `ProgramMenuFolder`, which translates to the Windows **Start** menu.

The `Shortcut` element has an `Id` attribute that uniquely identifies it within the installer, a `Name` attribute that defines what the shortcut will be called, and `Description` that provides an explanation about the shortcut's purpose, which the end user can see if they hover their mouse over it. The heart of the element is the `Target` attribute. This is what links our shortcut to the console application we're installing. In our example, the target points to the location of our installed `SampleApplication.exe` file, which it finds by referencing the `INSTALLFOLDER` directory surrounded by square brackets.

 You may also set `Target` to the `Id` of a `File` element preceded by a hash sign. For example, if the `File` element's `Id` had been `fileMyApp`, then we could use the following syntax for the `Target` attribute: `Target="[#fileMyApp]"`.

The `Shortcut` element's `Directory` attribute specifies where we'd like our shortcut to go. In this example, we set it to `Id` of our **Start** menu subfolder, `MyCompanyStartMenuFolder`.

We're required to add the `RemoveFolder` and `RegistryValue` elements to the component. The `RemoveFolder` element ensures that our new **Start** menu directory is removed during uninstallation. It has to do with handling the special case of cleaning up folders that were installed to a user's roaming profile. A roaming profile allows a user to take their applications with them, so to speak, when they log in to a computer other than their own, but still on the same network. More information about this requirement can be found at `http://msdn.microsoft.com/en-us/library/aa369011%28v=vs.85%29.aspx`.

The `RegistryValue` element serves as `KeyPath` for the component. To understand why, let's dig a little deeper into what it means to set something as `key-path`. Most of the time, a component contains a `File` element in it and that, by default, is `key-path`. This means that the Windows installer uses this file as the indicator to check whether the component is installed.

When it comes to shortcuts in the **Start** menu, we can't use a `File` element even if we had one in the same component as the shortcut. This is because, for software that's installed only for the current user, the `key-path` file may have been installed previously by another user on the same computer. For example, if user `Joe` installs the application first, then he will have created the application's files and a shortcut in his **Start** menu. Then, if user `Alice` logs in using her own Windows profile and installs the same software, Windows installer will see that that component is already present because it's checking the `File` element, which points to a shared component within `Program Files`—we'll get to how you shouldn't install to `Program Files` at all for per-user installations later. So, since the shortcut is in the same component as the file and the file is deemed installed already, `Alice` won't get a shortcut for her own **Start** menu.

The `Shortcut` element can't be `key-path` because it isn't really a file. It's just a link to a file. Often, when nothing else serves the purpose, we can mark the component itself as `key-path`. Doing so is shorthand for saying that the parent directory will be `key-path`. When it's a shared directory, such as a folder under `Program Files`, then that could cause the same problem as using a shared file for `key-path`.

The mandated solution is to add an entry to the current user's unique section of the Windows registry and have it be `key-path`. This way, it's obvious to the Windows installer that whether the component is installed depends on who the current user is. Why we can't use a user-specific directory as `key-path`, such as the current user's **Start** menu folder is hard to say. Regardless, the registry method is the only acceptable solution for the Windows installer.

 The `Package` element's `InstallScope` attribute determines whether an application will be installed for all users or just the current one. When set to `perMachine`, the application and its **Start** menu shortcuts will be installed for all users. When it's set to `perUser`, it will be installed for the current user only. Note that for per-user installations, we shouldn't add files to the `Program Files` folder because it requires elevated privileges to write to. We should use `LocalAppDataFolder` instead. However, the `ProgramMenuFolder` directory can be used for both per-machine and per-user installations. For per-machine scenarios, it automatically maps to the shared **Start** menu folder: `C:\ProgramData\Microsoft\Windows\Start Menu`. For per-user installations, it maps to a user-specific folder such as `C:\Users\Nick\AppData\Roaming\Microsoft\Windows\Start Menu`.

After running our installer, the end user will see a shortcut to our application in their **Start** menu:

There's more...

We can pass command-line arguments to our application when our shortcut is clicked. The following example uses the `Arguments` attribute to pass a single parameter, `ThisIsATest` to `SampleApplication.exe`:

```
<Shortcut Id="SampleApplicationShortcut"
    Name="Sample Application"
    Description="Runs the sample application"
    Target="[INSTALLFOLDER]SampleApplication.exe
    Arguments="ThisIsATest"
    Directory="MyCompanyStartMenuFolder" />
```

Our console application can now print the argument:

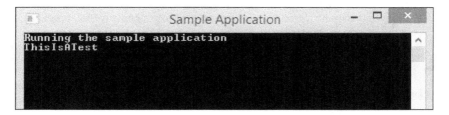

Adding an icon to a shortcut

Adding your own branded icons to your shortcuts will make them stand out. We can even have different icons for different purposes, such as one to denote the help documentation and another for a shortcut to the application itself. In this recipe, we'll see how to include an icon in our installer and have it displayed on a shortcut.

Getting ready

To prepare for this recipe, perform the following steps:

1. Create a new setup project and call it `IconShortcutInstaller`.

2. Set up your directory structure to include a folder in the **Start** menu:
   ```
   <Directory Id="TARGETDIR" Name="SourceDir">
     <Directory Id="ProgramFilesFolder">
       <Directory Id="INSTALLFOLDER" Name="My Company" />
     </Directory>
     <Directory Id="ProgramMenuFolder">
       <Directory Id="MyCompanyStartMenuFolder"
         Name="My Company" />
     </Directory>
   </Directory>
   ```

3. Include a text file named `Sample.txt` in the project and add a `Component` element to the `Product.wxs` file:

```
<ComponentGroup Id="ProductComponents"
    Directory="INSTALLFOLDER">
  <Component Id="cmpSampleTXT"
    Guid="{FED550CE-5F27-4729-B9D4-B6F71AABD4EE}">
    <File Id="fileSampleTXT" Source="Sample.txt" />
  </Component>
</ComponentGroup>
```

4. Choose an icon file (`.ico`) and add it to the project. In this recipe, we'll call it `logo.ico`.

 Various photo-editing software applications have a way to create an `.ico` file. For example, you can convert PNG to an icon in Photoshop by downloading the ICO format plugin at `http://www.telegraphics.com.au/sw/product/ICOFormat#icoformat`.

How to do it...

An `Icon` element that's placed inside a `Shortcut` will show up on that shortcut link after installation. The following steps will show you how to do it:

1. Add a component that contains the `Shortcut`, `RemoveFolder`, and `Registry` elements to install a shortcut to our `Sample.txt` file:

```
<Component Id="cmpShortcut"
    Guid="{14F99049-A277-45A9-B801-FB9F51CD5C5A}">
  <Shortcut Id="MyShortcut"
      Name="Sample Text"
      Description="Opens a text file"
      Directory="MyCompanyStartMenuFolder"
      Target="[#fileSampleTXT]">
  </Shortcut>

  <RemoveFolder Id="RemoveCompanyStartMenuFolder"
      Directory="MyCompanyStartMenuFolder"
      On="uninstall" />

  <RegistryValue Root="HKCU"
      Key="Software\My Company\Sample Application"
      Name="installed"
      Type="integer"
      Value="1"
      KeyPath="yes" />
</Component>
```

2. Inside the shortcut element, add an `Icon` element that references `logo.ico` with its `SourceFile` attribute:

```
<Shortcut ...>
  <Icon Id="MyShortcutIcon" SourceFile="logo.ico" />
</Shortcut>
```

How it works...

We began by adding a `Shortcut` element with a `Target` attribute that points to the `Id` of the `Sample.txt` file. The usual suspects that we discussed in the last recipe make an appearance including `RemoveFolder` and `RegistryValue`. These are required elements that ensure that the shortcut is removed during uninstall and that there's an element to serve as `key-path` for the component.

To add an icon to our shortcut, we simply introduce an `Icon` element. Its `Id` attribute uniquely identifies the icon within the MSI and its `SourceFile` attribute references a `.ico` file to use. After running our installer, the user will see our icon on the shortcut:

There's more...

Another way to add an icon to a shortcut is to use the `Shortcut` element's `Icon` attribute. This can reference any `Icon` element in your project by `Id`. So, you can place an `Icon` element in another `Fragment`, as follows:

```
<Fragment>
  <Icon Id="MyShortcutIcon" SourceFile="logo.ico" />
</Fragment>
```

Next, reference this element's `Id` attribute with the `Shortcut` element's `Icon` attribute:

```
<Shortcut Id="MyShortcut"
          Name="Sample Text"
          Description="Opens a text file"
          Directory="MyCompanyStartMenuFolder"
          Target="[#fileSampleTXT]"
          Icon="MyShortcutIcon">
```

This can come in handy if you prefer to define all of your icon resources in a separate fragment for better modularity.

Placing a shortcut on the desktop

The **Start** menu is the best place to place application shortcuts because it keeps them organized and users only see them when they want to. The desktop comes in second though, displaying a user's favorite links front and center.

In this recipe, we'll place a shortcut to our `Sample.txt` file on the user's desktop. As we've discussed previously, who will see this shortcut depends on the value of the `Package` element's `InstallScope` attribute. When it's set to `perMachine`, all users will see the shortcut. When set to `perUser`, it will be installed only for the current user.

Getting ready

To prepare for this recipe, perform the following steps:

1. Create a new setup project and name it `DesktopShortcutInstaller`.

2. Include a text file named `Sample.txt` in the project and add a `Component` element to the `Product.wxs` file:

```
<ComponentGroup Id="ProductComponents"
                Directory="INSTALLFOLDER">
  <Component Id="cmpSampleTXT"
             Guid="{EB57CD24-8DEE-41EC-8E3C-F9B6DF94B34D}">
    <File Id="fileSampleTXT" Source="Sample.txt" />
  </Component>
</ComponentGroup>
```

How to do it...

Add a `Directory` element that points to the `Desktop` folder and then reference it in a `Shortcut` element. The following steps will show you how to do it:

1. Add a new `Directory` element that has an `Id` of `DesktopFolder`:

```
<Directory Id="TARGETDIR" Name="SourceDir">
  <Directory Id="ProgramFilesFolder">
    <Directory Id="INSTALLFOLDER" Name="My Company" />
  </Directory>
  <Directory Id="DesktopFolder" />
</Directory>
```

2. Add a `Component` containing a `Shortcut` element that has a `Directory` attribute set to `DesktopFolder`:

```
<Component Id="cmpDesktopShortcut"
            Guid="{882D728B-F837-4C06-8BD7-69E9ABE51176}">
  <Shortcut Id="MyDesktopShortcut"
            Name="Sample Text"
            Description="Opens a text file"
            Directory="DesktopFolder"
            Target="[#fileSampleTXT] " />
</Component>
```

3. Within that same component, add a `RegistryValue` element to serve as `KeyPath` for `Component`. Unlike other shortcuts you've created, you do not need to add a `RemoveFolder` element:

```
<Component ...>
  <Shortcut ... />
  <RegistryValue Root="HKCU"
      Key="Software\My Company\Sample Application"
      Name="installed"
      Type="integer"
      Value="1"
      KeyPath="yes" />
</Component>
```

How it works...

We can access the `Desktop` folder by adding a `Directory` element with `Id` of `DesktopFolder`:

```
<Directory Id="DesktopFolder" />
```

If we're installing our application for all users, then our shortcut will appear on the desktop of every user that logs on to the computer. The setting that controls whether we are installing for all users is the `Package` element's `InstallScope` attribute. A value of `perMachine` will install for all users, whereas a value of `perUser` will install only for the current user:

```
<Package InstallerVersion="200"
    Compressed="yes"
    InstallScope="perMachine" />
```

The `Shortcut` element's `Target` attribute points to the file to be opened when the user clicks on the shortcut. Note that for this example I chose to use the `[#fileSampleTXT]` syntax, which points to the `Id` of the `File` element. The `Directory` attribute sets where the shortcut will be created. When the user runs our installer, a link to `Sample.txt` is added to their desktop:

Creating a shortcut to a folder

In this recipe, we will create a shortcut to a folder and place it on the **Start** menu. Having a shortcut to a folder makes it easy to get to child files and subfolders without having a shortcut for each one. For example, if we're installing a suite of developer tools, we might provide a link to a folder of sample projects. The shortcut will open the Windows file explorer so the user can browse through the projects with ease. This also makes it easy for us to change what's in that folder without worrying too much about updating the shortcuts.

We'll add a folder for logfiles under the `C:\ProgramData` folder, which is a machine-level folder that's meant to store things such as logs, configuration settings, and other dynamic files. To make things simple, we'll install our log files folder as an empty directory. Recall that we'll need to use the `CreateFolder` element to ensure that the Windows installer adds the directory even though it's empty.

Getting ready

To prepare for this recipe, perform the following steps:

1. Create a new setup project and name it `FolderShortcutInstaller`.

2. Set up a hierarchy of `Directory` elements. The following markup will create a folder on the **Start** menu by referencing `ProgramMenuFolder` and another folder at `C:\ProgramData\My Company\Log Files` by referencing `CommonAppDataFolder`:

```
<Directory Id="TARGETDIR" Name="SourceDir">
  <Directory Id="ProgramMenuFolder">
    <Directory Id="MyCompanyStartMenuFolder"
               Name="My Company" />
  </Directory>
```

```
<Directory Id="CommonAppDataFolder">
  <Directory Id="MyAppDataFolder" Name="My Company">
    <Directory Id="MyLogFiles" Name="Log Files" />
  </Directory>
</Directory>
</Directory>
```

How to do it...

Set the `Shortcut` element's `Directory` attribute to the `Id` of the target `Directory` element. The following steps will show you how to do it:

1. We will begin with installing an empty folder. To do this, add a `CreateFolder` element within a component. Use its `Directory` attribute to identify the directory that we're creating:

```
<ComponentGroup Id="ProductComponents"
     Directory="MyLogFiles">
  <Component Id="cmpMyFolderShortcut"
     Guid="{350D8A0D-4CF8-4129-A441-22BF80D97407}">
    <CreateFolder Directory="MyLogFiles" />
  </Component>
</ComponentGroup>
```

2. Within that same component, add a `Shortcut` element that uses its `Target` attribute to point to the `MyLogFiles` directory. Its `Directory` attribute specifies that the shortcut will be created within our **Start** menu folder:

```
<Component ...>
  <CreateFolder ... />
  <Shortcut Id="cmpLogFolderShortcut"
     Name="Log Files"
     Description="Opens log files folder"
     Directory="MyCompanyStartMenuFolder"
     Target="[MyLogFiles]" />
</Component>
```

3. Add the `RemoveFolder` and `RegistryValue` elements to the component, so that our **Start** menu folder will be removed during uninstallation and we have a value in the registry to serve as `key-path` for the component:

```
<Component ...>
  <CreateFolder ... />
  <Shortcut ... />

  <RemoveFolder Id="RemoveCompanyStartMenuFolder"
     Directory="MyCompanyStartMenuFolder"
```

```
                    On="uninstall" />

        <RegistryValue Root="HKCU"
            Key="Software\My Company\Sample Application"
            Name="installed"
            Type="integer"
            Value="1"
            KeyPath="yes" />
    </Component>
```

How it works...

We started by creating a directory under `C:\ProgramData` that we could later add a shortcut for. In our hypothetical scenario, this folder could be used to store logfiles that the application generates. Since, at the time of installation, there won't be any log files yet, we added a `CreateFolder` element to the component so that the folder will be created even though it's empty.

We set the `Shortcut` element's `Target` attribute so that it references our `MyLogFiles` directory. After running our installer, we'll see a link to our `Log Files` directory on the **Start** menu, which, when clicked, will open the Windows file explorer:

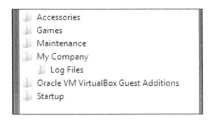

Creating an advertised shortcut that installs a feature on demand

Ordinarily, when the end user executes one of our installers, all of the components get installed right away. However, when a component is tied to an advertised shortcut, it isn't installed until the user clicks the shortcut that the associated file gets installed. This type of shortcut provides a sort of install-on-demand functionality. You might use it to delay the installation of a feature that many users wouldn't use right away, such as supplementary tools or sample projects.

Getting ready

To prepare for this recipe, perform the following steps:

1. Create a setup project and name it `AdvertisedShortcutInstaller`.

2. Add a **C# Console Application** project to the same Visual Studio solution and call it `SampleApplication`. We will include this in our installer, paired with an advertised shortcut so that it won't be installed until the user clicks on the shortcut. Add the following code to its `Program.cs` file:

```csharp
using System;

namespace SampleApplication
{
  public class Program
  {
    public static void Main(string[] args)
    {
      Console.WriteLine("Running the sample application.");
      Console.ReadKey();
    }
  }
}
```

3. Reference the console application project in the setup project and then add a `Component` element to include it in the installation:

```xml
<ComponentGroup Id="AdvertisedComponents"
    Directory="INSTALLFOLDER">
  <Component Id="cmpSampleApplication"
    Guid="{3F213CF5-6402-4090-9E3E-5E3F4FCA3148}">
    <File Source="$(var.SampleApplication.TargetDir)
SampleApplication.exe" />
  </Component>
</ComponentGroup>
```

How to do it...

Update the `Feature` element so that it allows advertisement and include an advertised shortcut so that its components are installed on demand. The following steps will show you how:

1. Identify the feature that your advertised components will be included in, and set its `AllowAdvertise` attribute to `yes` and its `TypicalDefault` attribute to `advertise`:

```xml
<Feature Id="MyAdvertisedFeature"
    Title="Advertised Components"
    Level="1"
```

```
      AllowAdvertise="yes"
      TypicalDefault="advertise">
   <ComponentGroupRef Id="AdvertisedComponents"/>
</Feature>
```

2. Define your `Directory` structure so that it includes a folder within `ProgramFilesFolder`, since that is where our console application will be installed, and `ProgramMenuFolder` to place our shortcut on the **Start** menu:

```
<Directory Id="TARGETDIR" Name="SourceDir">
   <Directory Id="ProgramFilesFolder">
      <Directory Id="INSTALLFOLDER" Name="My Company" />
   </Directory>
   <Directory Id="ProgramMenuFolder">
      <Directory Id="MyCompanyStartMenuDirectory"
                Name="My Company" />
   </Directory>
</Directory>
```

3. Within that same component as our `SampleApplication.exe`, add a `Shortcut` element. Set its `Advertise` attribute to `yes` and its `Directory` attribute to the `Id` of our **Start** menu directory. You should omit the `Target` attribute:

```
<Component Id="cmpSampleApplication" ...>

   <File ... />


   <Shortcut Id="MyAdvertisedShortcut"
             Name="Install the Sample Application (optional)"
             Description="Installs advertised app"
             Directory="MyCompanyStartMenuDirectory"
             Advertise="yes" />

</Component>
```

4. Add a `RemoveFolder` element to the component so that our custom Start menu directory will be removed during uninstallation. We do not need to add a `RegistryValue` element:

```
<Component ...>
   <File ... />
   <Shortcut ... />
```

```
<RemoveFolder Id="RemoveMyShortcutDir"
    On="uninstall"
    Directory="MyCompanyStartMenuDirectory"/>
</Component>
```

How it works...

The first thing we did was add the `AllowAdvertise` attribute to our `Feature` element so that it could support advertised components. We also set its `TypicalDefault` attribute to `advertise` so that advertisement was turned on. In this example, we included one file, `SampleApplication.exe`, in this feature. It won't be installed until the shortcut is clicked.

You may be wondering, "Do I need to associate every component that I'd like to install on demand with an advertised shortcut?" Nope. You only need one shortcut for the entire feature. Every other `Component` that's included in that feature will also be advertised. In other words, advertisement happens at the `Feature` level. When the shortcut is clicked, all of the components in that feature will be installed. Prior to that, none of them will be. If you want to install other components immediately, they'll have to go into a separate, non-advertised feature.

To create the advertised shortcut, we added a `Shortcut` element to the same component as the `File` element and set its `Advertise` attribute to `yes`. This will set up the shortcut as the trigger to install all components within the feature.

When the user runs our installer, the shortcut will be added to their **Start** menu:

At this point, if you were to look in `Program Files`, you wouldn't see our console application or even the folder it goes into. It isn't until we click on the shortcut that the file and its parent folder get installed.

There's more...

One caveat to advertising a feature is that it relies on running the MSI a second time. So, say you copy the MSI package to your desktop, install it, but wait to click on the advertised shortcut. For now, none of the advertised components are installed. Later, you click on the shortcut but by then you've deleted the MSI from your desktop. You'll be greeted with the following error message:

The advertised shortcut tries to execute the MSI again to install the missing components. However, it relies on the package being in the same place as it was before. One way to solve this problem is to include the installer in a WiX Bootstrapper project. Bootstrappers keep their MSI packages in a cache on the user's computer. This behavior will ensure that our installer will always be present when it's needed by an advertised shortcut. So, if you're considering using advertisement, you may be better off pairing it with a bootstrapper.

5
Editing XML Files during Installation

In this chapter, we will cover the following recipes:

- Adding a new element to an XML file during installation
- Setting the value of an attribute on an XML element
- Inserting inner text into an XML element
- Adding an XML element only if it does not already exist
- Removing an XML element

Introduction

Part of setting up an application is making sure that it's configured correctly for the environment where it will run. For example, if we're installing to a development machine, we'd set up our database connection strings differently than if we're installing to production. With WiX, we can install an XML configuration file and then transform it on the fly.

In this chapter, we'll see several transformations that you can perform on XML, including adding and removing elements, adding attributes and inner text, and creating an element only if it doesn't already exist. All of these functionalities come from a versatile element called `XmlConfig` that can be found in the WiX `UtilExtension` namespace.

You might be wondering how using WiX to transform an XML file at installation time stacks up against the alternatives. One is to keep separate configuration files for each environment. The benefit of this approach is that it's easy to start off with. It doesn't take much to copy one file into a `DEV` folder and another into a `PROD` folder. The downside comes later as new settings are added and you find yourself having to keep the two files in sync. The task becomes more difficult as you add new environments that have their own subtle configuration differences, especially if different teams are responsible for updating their own versions of the file.

Another alternative, if you're building an ASP.NET web application, is to use the `Web.config` transformation feature that became available with Visual Studio 2010. It allows you to associate a transform file with a particular build configuration, such as `Web.Debug.config` for a debug build. When you build in debug mode, `Web.config` will be updated to reflect the debug transforms. The benefit of this is that there's Visual Studio support and the transforms can be viewed in **Solution Explorer**. The downside is that it only works with ASP.NET and you have to maintain a different build configuration for each environment that you want to deploy to.

The WiX transforms described here are versatile in that they can update any type of XML file and they avoid the trap of having to maintain a distinct configuration file for each environment. You can store a single file, without having to change build configurations, and simply transform it during deployment to suit the needs of the environment. However, a disadvantage is that the transforms are tucked away in a setup project, so it may not be obvious to everyone on the team how they're being set. Weigh the pros and cons and see what's best for you.

Adding a new element to an XML file during installation

In this recipe, we'll learn how to add an element to an XML file. One place where this might be useful is to enable tracing in an ASP.NET web application. Tracing lets you see diagnostic information about a running web application. We'll start with a basic `Web.config` file that doesn't have any tracing configuration in it and add a `trace` element to set it up.

Getting ready

To prepare for this recipe, perform the following steps:

1. Create a new setup project and name it `XmlElementInstaller`.

2. So that we'll have something to modify, add an XML file to the project and call it `Web.config`. Add the following markup to it:

```
<?xml version="1.0"?>
<configuration>
  <appSettings />
```

```
  <connectionStrings />

  <system.web>
    <authentication mode="Windows" />
  </system.web>
</configuration>
```

3. Add a Component element to `Product.wxs` to include the file in the installation:

```
<ComponentGroup Id="ProductComponents"
                Directory="INSTALLFOLDER">
  <Component Id="cmpWebCONFIG"
             Guid="{64147F6A-BD21-414A-83DA-70855B615353}">
    <File Source="Web.config" />
  </Component>
</ComponentGroup>
```

How to do it...

Add an `XmlConfig` element with its `Node` attribute set to `document` and its inner text set to the element that you'd like to create. Perform the following steps:

1. Add `UtilExtension` to the project by right-clicking on the `References` node in **Solution Explorer** and going to **Add Reference** | **WixUtilExtension.dll** | **Add** | **OK**.

2. Add the `UtilExtension` namespace to your `Wix` element:

```
<Wix xmlns="http://schemas.microsoft.com/wix/2006/wi"
    xmlns:util="http://schemas.microsoft.com/wix/UtilExtension">
```

3. Add a component that contains `util:XmlConfig`. Set the `XmlConfig` element's `Node` attribute to `document` to insert new XML content into the specified file. Its inner text defines the new element and its attributes, while its `ElementPath` tells WiX where it will go within the existing markup. Be sure to mark the `Component` as `KeyPath`:

```
<Component Id="cmpAddTracing"
           Guid="{07A2DF2B-B5AF-4277-9304-4D6CAEBF7BD5}"
           KeyPath="yes">
  <util:XmlConfig Id="addTracing"
                  File="[INSTALLFOLDER]Web.config"
                  Action="create"
                  On="install"
                  Node="document"
                  ElementPath="//configuration/system.web"
                  Sequence="1">
    <![CDATA[<trace enabled="true" />]]>
  </util:XmlConfig>
</Component>
```

How it works...

The `UtilExtension` namespace contains an element called `XmlConfig` that has everything we need to interact with an XML document. We'll be using it throughout the chapter; however, in this case, we're using it to add an element called `trace` to the `system.web` section of the configuration file.

To begin with, we use the `File` element to install our `Web.config` file to the end user's computer. The order of an installation goes like this: first the XML file is copied to its target directory and then our `XmlConfig` element gets a chance to update that file after it has been installed. If there's more than one `XmlConfig` element in the project, we can control the order in which their changes are applied by setting each one's `Sequence` attribute.

The `XmlConfig` element's `File` attribute identifies the path to the file we're going to update. By setting its `Action` attribute to `create` and its `Node` attribute to `document`, we're saying that we want to add some new content to the file. We define that content within the `XmlConfig` element as its inner text. `ElementPath` sets where to create the new content: within the `Web.config` file. It uses the XPath syntax; you can learn more about this at `http://www.w3schools.com/xpath/xpath_syntax.asp`.

When we run our installer, the `Web.config` file will be copied to its directory and, when all is said and done, our `trace` element will have been added inside the `system.web` element:

```xml
<?xml version="1.0"?>
<configuration>
  <appSettings/>
  <connectionStrings/>

  <system.web>
    <authentication mode="Windows"/>
    <trace enabled="true"/>
  </system.web>
</configuration>
```

There's more...

There's another advantage to adding an element at installation time. We might choose to add the element, or not add it, depending on some condition that can only be discerned during the installation. By adding `Condition` within the same `Component` element as our `XmlConfig` element, we can add a rule that decides whether or not to add the element.

For example, if we only wanted to create the XML element if we're in a `DEV` environment, we could start by adding a property to our `Product.wxs` file as follows:

```xml
<Property Id="ENVIRONMENT" Value="DEV" />
```

In a real-world scenario, the value of this property will probably be set by the user through an install wizard. Nevertheless, the following `Condition` element checks the property to see whether we should execute the XML transformation:

```
<Component Id="cmpAddTracing"
           Guid="{07A2DF2B-B5AF-4277-9304-4D6CAEBF7BD5}"
           KeyPath="yes">
  <util:XmlConfig Id="addTracing"
                  File="[INSTALLFOLDER]Web.config"
                  Action="create"
                  On="install"
                  Node="element"
                  Name="trace"
                  ElementPath="//configuration/system.web"
                  Sequence="1">
    <![CDATA[<trace enabled="true" />]]>
  </util:XmlConfig>

  <Condition><![CDATA[ENVIRONMENT = "DEV"]]></Condition>
</Component>
```

Now, if we're installing somewhere other than `DEV`, such as to `PROD`, `Web.config` will not be updated with the new element.

Setting the value of an attribute on an XML element

Although settings can often be configured by adding entire elements, others can be configured by setting an attribute on an already existing element. For example, we can replace a default database connection string by setting the `connectionString` attribute on an `add` element. By doing it at installation time, we're given the flexibility to collect the connection details from the user or base them on the environment in which the installer is running. In this recipe, we'll see how to use the `XmlConfig` element to change a default connection string to something else.

Getting ready

To prepare for this recipe, perform the following steps:

1. Create a new setup project and name it `XmlAttributeInstaller`.

2. Add an XML file to the project and call it `Web.config`. Add the following markup to it:

```
<?xml version="1.0"?>
<configuration>
  <appSettings />
```

```
<connectionStrings>
  <add name="mydb" providerName="System.Data.SqlClient"
connectionString="Data Source=devserver\MYDATABASE; Initial
Catalog=Customers; Integrated Security=SSPI" />
</connectionStrings>

<system.web>
  <authentication mode="Windows" />
</system.web>
</configuration>
```

3. Add a `Component` element to `Product.wxs` to include the file in the installation:

```
<ComponentGroup Id="ProductComponents"
                Directory="INSTALLFOLDER">
  <Component Id="cmpWebCONFIG"
             Guid="{5812219F-D6B0-4AE8-A205-3E528D5006E5}">
    <File Source="Web.config" />
  </Component>
</ComponentGroup>
```

How to do it...

Update an `XML` attribute by setting an `XmlConfig` element's `Node` attribute to `value`, its `Name` to the name of the attribute to be set, and its `Value` to the string to be used:

1. Add `UtilExtension` to the project by right-clicking on the `References` node in **Solution Explorer** and going to **Add Reference | WixUtilExtension.dll | Add | OK**.

2. Add the `UtilExtension` namespace to your `Wix` element:

```
<Wix xmlns="http://schemas.microsoft.com/wix/2006/wi"
     xmlns:util="http://schemas.microsoft.com/wix/UtilExtension">
```

3. The default connection string in `Web.config` uses `devserver\MYDATABASE` as its datasource. We'll define a property to fill in the server at installation time. Add the following line to your `Product.wxs` file:

```
<Property Id="DB_INSTANCE" Value="prodserver\MYDATABASE" />
```

4. Add a component with an `XmlConfig` element inside it to update the `connectionString` attribute within our `Web.config` file. Instead of pointing to `devserver\MYDATABASE`, it will point to `prodserver\MYDATABASE`. Be sure to mark the component as `KeyPath`:

```
<Component Id="cmpUpdateSampleXML"
    Guid="{CE1F79BC-337A-44FA-9D41-7825564B5CC8}"
    KeyPath="yes">
```

```
        <util:XmlConfig Id="setConnString"
            File="[INSTALLFOLDER]Web.config"
            Action="create"
            On="install"
            Node="value"
            Name="connectionString"
            Value="Data Source=[DB_INSTANCE]; Initial Catalog=Customers;
    Integrated Security=SSPI" ElementPath="//configuration/
    connectionStrings/add[\[]@name='mydb'[\]]"
            Sequence="1" />
    </Component>
```

How it works...

Our Web.config file starts out with an add element that has an attribute called connectionString pointing to devserver\MYDATABASE. In order to update this value to prodserver\MYDATABASE at installation time, we include a component that contains an XmlConfig element, whose ElementPath uses an XPath statement to find the add element:

```
ElementPath="//configuration/connectionStrings/add[\[]@
name='mydb'[\]]"
```

The syntax here has one little quirk that differentiates it from your garden-variety XPath. Ordinarily, if you wanted to find the add element that has a name attribute of mydb, you'd append the following to your XPath:

```
add[@name='mydb']
```

In WiX, it looks like this:

```
add[\[]@name='mydb'[\]]
```

That's because the ElementPath attribute might make use of WiX properties. For example, suppose we'd defined a Property named DB_NAME as follows:

```
<Property Id="DB_NAME" Value="mydb" />
```

We could then dynamically change which add element we're looking for by inserting this property into ElementPath with the following code snippet:

```
add[\[]@name='[DB_NAME]'[\]]
```

As you can see, by surrounding the name of the property with square brackets, we're able to substitute in its value. The DB_NAME property will be replaced with the value mydb. The other square brackets that aren't directly surrounding the WiX property are meant to be parsed by XPath and must be escaped so that there's no confusion. The way in which Windows Installer escapes square brackets is by using [\[] instead of [and [\]] instead of].

Now, you'll notice that the `connectionString` attribute is made up of three key-value pairs: `Data Source`, `Initial Catalog`, and `Integrated Security`. Our `XmlConfig` element will replace the whole string, but because we're only interested in changing the data source and can keep the rest the same, we can insert a `DB_INSTANCE` property for just that key-value pair:

```
Data Source=[DB_INSTANCE]; Initial Catalog=Customers; Integrated
Security=SSPI
```

When the end user runs our installer, the `connectionStrings` sections of our `Web.config` file will be updated to the following:

```
<connectionStrings>
  <add name="mydb" providerName="System.Data.SqlClient"
connectionString="Data Source=prodserver\MYDATABASE; Initial
Catalog=Customers; Integrated Security=SSPI" />
</connectionStrings>
```

Inserting inner text into an XML element

In some cases, an XML file might use the inner text of an element to configure a setting. For example, if you view the properties of an ASP.NET project, there's a **Settings** tab where you can add rows of named application settings:

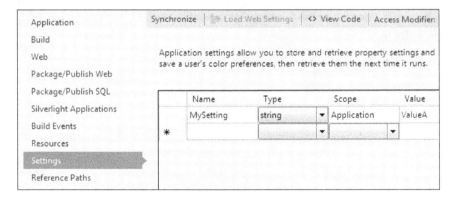

These settings will be stored in `Web.config` under the `applicationSettings` node:

```
<configuration>
  <!--Other elements omitted for brevity-->

  <applicationSettings>
    <MyWebApp.Properties.Settings>
      <setting name="MySetting" serializeAs="String">
        <value>ValueA</value>
```

```
      </setting>
    </MyWebApp.Properties.Settings>
  </applicationSettings>
</configuration>
```

As you can see, the value of the setting is stored as inner text in an element called `value`. In this recipe, we'll update this inner text so that instead of saying `ValueA`, it will say `ValueB`.

Getting ready

To prepare for this recipe, perform the following steps:

1. Create a new setup project and name it `XmlInnerTextInstaller`.

2. So that we'll have something to modify, add an XML file to the project and name it `Web.config`. Add the following markup to it:

    ```xml
    <?xml version="1.0"?>
    <configuration>
      <applicationSettings>
        <MyWebApp.Properties.Settings>
          <setting name="MySetting" serializeAs="String">
            <value>ValueA</value>
          </setting>
        </MyWebApp.Properties.Settings>
      </applicationSettings>
    </configuration>
    ```

3. Add a `Component` element to `Product.wxs` to include the file in the installation:

    ```xml
    <Component Id="cmpWebCONFIG"
        Guid="{1B527456-4367-4D3D-AAE4-7E5C22FB9192}">
      <File Source="Web.config" />
    </Component>
    ```

How to do it...

Set the `XmlConfig` element's `Node` attribute to value and its `Value` attribute to the text you'd like to insert as inner text. Perform the following steps to do so:

1. Add `UtilExtension` to the project by right-clicking on the `References` node in **Solution Explorer** and going to **Add Reference | WixUtilExtension.dll | Add | OK**.

2. Add the `UtilExtension` namespace to the `Wix` element:

    ```xml
    <Wix xmlns="http://schemas.microsoft.com/wix/2006/wi"
      xmlns:util="http://schemas.microsoft.com/wix/UtilExtension">
    ```

3. Add a component, making sure to mark it with the `KeyPath` attribute; within that element, add an `XmlConfig` element that has a `Node` attribute of `value` and its `Value` attribute set to the inner text you'd like to use:

```
<Component Id="cmpSetInnerText"
  Guid="{C96824AC-1BC9-44A9-94AF-92218C341797}"
  KeyPath="yes">
  <util:XmlConfig Id="setInnerText"
    File="[INSTALLFOLDER]Web.config"
    Action="create"
    On="install"
    Node="value"
    Value="ValueB" ElementPath="//configuration/
applicationSettings/MyWebApp.Properties.Settings/setting[\[]@
name='MySetting'[\]]/value"
    Sequence="1" />
</Component>
```

How it works...

We began in the usual way by adding a reference to `UtilExtension` so that we will have access to the `XmlConfig` element. The syntax to add inner text to an XML element is a lot like adding a value to an attribute, but in this case we omit the `Name` attribute. Setting `Action` to `create` and `Node` to `value` but omitting the `Name` attribute means that we'll be creating inner text. `ElementPath` identifies the element to add inner text to and `Value` sets the `text` to add.

After running the installer, the `value` element's inner text, which was `ValueA`, will be replaced with `ValueB`. The updated XML file now contains the following:

```
<setting name="MySetting" serializeAs="String">
  <value>ValueB</value>
</setting>
```

There's more...

In the previous example, we added a simple string inside of the `value` element. We can also insert more complex content, such as elements within elements and elements containing their own inner text. First, remove the `Value` attribute from the `XmlConfig` element and change the `Node` attribute to `document`. Then, add any XML markup that you'd like to include inside of the `XmlConfig` element. The following example adds `<myElement>This is a test</myElement>` as the inner text of the target element:

```
<util:XmlConfig Id="updateSomeXML"
    File="[INSTALLFOLDER]SomeFile.xml"
```

```
    Action="create"
    On="install"
    Node="document" ElementPath="//parent/child[\[]@
name='section1'[\]]"
    Sequence="1">
  <![CDATA[<myElement>This is a test</myElement>]]>
</util:XmlConfig>
```

Adding an XML element only if it does not already exist

In this recipe, we'll learn a technique of adding an XML element only if it isn't already present. When updating a configuration file that's shared amongst applications, such as the machine-level `Web.config` file, you might use this to keep old user settings intact or else create them anew if they aren't already set. For this recipe, we'll check for the existence of an element called `add` with a `key` attribute of `UserSetting1` and add it if it isn't already there.

Getting ready

To prepare for this recipe, perform the following steps:

1. Create a new setup project and call it `XmlElementExistsInstaller`.

2. Add an XML file called `Web.config` with the following markup:

```
<?xml version="1.0"?>
<configuration>
  <appSettings>
    <add key="UserSetting1" value="abc" />
  </appSettings>
</configuration>
```

3. Add a `Component` element to `Product.wxs` to include the file in the installation:

```
<ComponentGroup Id="ProductComponents"
                Directory="INSTALLFOLDER">
  <Component Id="cmpWebCONFIG"
             Guid="{1B527456-4367-4D3D-AAE4-7E5C22FB9192}">
    <File Source="Web.config" />
  </Component>
</ComponentGroup>
```

How to do it...

Use the `XmlConfig` element's `VerifyPath` attribute to check for the existence of an element before adding it:

1. Add `UtilExtension` to the project by right-clicking on the `References` node in **Solution Explorer** and going to **Add Reference | WixUtilExtension.dll | Add | OK**.

2. Add the `UtilExtension` namespace to the `Wix` element:

```
<Wix xmlns="http://schemas.microsoft.com/wix/2006/wi"
   xmlns:util="http://schemas.microsoft.com/wix/UtilExtension">
```

3. Add a component with an `XmlConfig` element that uses its `VerifyPath` attribute to check whether the element exists before adding it:

```
<Component Id="cmpAddSettingIfNotExist"
          Guid="{6E92CD4E-1173-4D60-B7EE-49613FC42632}"
          KeyPath="yes">
  <util:XmlConfig Id="addSettingIfNotExist"
                  File="[INSTALLFOLDER]Web.config"
                  Action="create"
                  On="install"
                  Node="document"
                  ElementPath="//configuration/appSettings"
VerifyPath="//configuration/appSettings/add[\[]@
key='UserSetting1'[\]]">
     <![CDATA[<add key="UserSetting1" value="def" />]]>
  </util:XmlConfig>
</Component>
```

How it works...

Setting `Action` to `create` and `Node` to `document` but omitting the `Name` attribute means that we'll be inserting inner text into an existing element. In this case, we're adding our `<add key="UserSetting1" value="def" />` application setting.

`ElementPath` is an XPath expression that locates the node that we'd like to add an element to. The `VerifyPath` attribute checks for a matching path in the document. In this example, we're checking for an `add` element that has a key of `UserSetting1`. If it doesn't exist, then the XML we've added inside the `XmlConfig` element will be created. However, if there's already `UserSetting1`, then we won't overwrite it.

Removing an XML element

In this recipe, we'll see how to remove an element from an XML document. You might use this when updating a shared configuration file that has a setting that no longer applies. We'll start out with a configuration file that has three add elements in it. During our installation, we'll remove the middle one.

Getting ready

To prepare for this recipe, perform the following steps:

1. Create a new setup project and call it RemoveElementInstaller.

2. Add an XML file named Web.config to the project and add the following markup to it:

```
<?xml version="1.0"?>
<configuration>
  <appSettings>
    <add key="UserSetting1" value="abc" />
    <add key="UserSetting2" value="def" />
    <add key="UserSetting3" value="ghi" />
  </appSettings>
</configuration>
```

3. Add a Component element to Product.wxs to include the file in the install:

```
<Component Id="cmpWebCONFIG"
           Guid="{1B527456-4367-4D3D-AAE4-7E5C22FB9192}
  <File Source="Web.config" />
</Component>
```

How to do it...

Set the XmlConfig element's Action to delete and use its ElementPath and VerifyPath attributes to locate the element to remove:

1. Add UtilExtension to the project by right-clicking on the References node in **Solution Explorer** and going to **Add Reference | WixUtilExtension.dll | Add | OK**.

2. Add the UtilExtension namespace to the Wix element:

```
<Wix xmlns="http://schemas.microsoft.com/wix/2006/wi"
     xmlns:util="http://schemas.microsoft.com/wix/UtilExtension">
```

3. Add an `XmlConfig` element with an `Action` attribute set to `delete` to remove an element from the XML file. Use the `VerifyPath` attribute to specify which element to delete:

```
<Component Id="cmpRemoveElement"
           Guid="{71A5AE3D-7D1A-4CA2-8E82-081CF3A1F9C8}"
           KeyPath="yes">
  <util:XmlConfig Id="removeElement"
                  File="[INSTALLFOLDER]Web.config"
                  Action="delete"
                  On="install"
                  Node="element"
                  ElementPath="//configuration/appSettings"
VerifyPath="//configuration/appSettings/add[\[]@
key='UserSetting2'[\]]"
                  Sequence="1" />
</Component>
```

How it works...

Setting the `XmlConfig` element's `Action` to `delete` and `Node` to `element` means that we'll be removing an element from the XML file. The `ElementPath` points to the parent node of the element we want to delete and `VerifyPath` identifies the element itself.

After running the installer, our `Web.config` file will contain the following markup, where the middle element that had a key of `UserSetting2` has been removed:

```
<?xml version="1.0"?>
<configuration>
  <appSettings>
    <add key="UserSetting1" value="abc" />

    <add key="UserSetting3" value="ghi" />
  </appSettings>
</configuration>
```

Note that if the element that we're removing has child elements, they'll also be removed.

6
Custom Actions

In this chapter, we will cover the following recipes:

- ▸ Creating a C# custom action and referencing it in your project
- ▸ Passing information entered by a user to a deferred custom action
- ▸ Preventing custom action data from being displayed in the install log
- ▸ Running an executable as a custom action without showing a console window by using CAQuietExec
- ▸ Testing rollback custom actions with WixFailWhenDeferred

Introduction

An MSI installer has three distinct phases. The first, which is called the *UI sequence*, shows a graphical user interface (if you don't have one, this phase will go really fast). During this phase, the user can enter their preferences for things such as where the files will be installed, which features to include, and whether the user accepts the end user license agreement. No changes are made to the system at this point; we're just collecting information.

The next stage is called the immediate phase of the execute sequence, and this is where the installer thinks about all of the changes that it's going to make to the computer. It makes a list, so that it knows how to do that work in an orderly fashion and also how to undo it if an error occurs. After all, the last thing we want to do is leave the user's computer in a halfway state where only part of the installation took place. It's much better to undo the whole thing. This immediate phase is the first thing to happen after the user has clicked on the **Install** button.

The third phase is called *the deferred phase of the execute sequence*. This is when all of the system-modifying actions take place. This includes creating new files and folders, updating registry keys, and anything else that the installer planned to do when it made its list during the immediate stage. If one of these actions fails, the whole script will be run in reverse order, thereby reverting any changes. Otherwise, if nothing goes wrong, we get to the end and the user is shown a dialog that says everything went okay.

Windows installer comes with the knowledge of how to do all of the basic stuff, which includes installing files, creating shortcuts, and writing to the registry, along with how to undo these actions if a rollback occurs. So, what can we do when we need to do something out of the norm? How do we perform some custom action during one of the three phases? The answer is to write some new markup or code and have it included in one the sequences.

You can write custom actions in several ways. For basic stuff, such as changing the path of a directory during installation, there are XML elements in place that we can leverage. In this chapter, we'll focus on more complex scenarios that involve writing our actions as C# code. For actions that change the user's system, we'll need to author our actions so that there's a compensating action to roll it back if there's an error. We'll also take a look at gotcha, such as how to pass data that the user entered during the UI sequence to an action that happens during the deferred stage of the execute sequence. You can't just send the data, you have to do it in a special way. Although we'll be using C#, custom actions can also be written using VB.NET or C++.

Creating a C# custom action and referencing it in your project

In this recipe, we'll see how to create a C# custom action that does something simple: get the computer's time zone and store it in a WiX property. Often, we need to collect information like this and either present it on the GUI or use it behind the scenes to make some decisions later when the computer is modified.

Windows installer doesn't know how to use a C# custom action directly. It only understands unmanaged code. However, WiX comes with a library called **Deployment Tools Foundation (DTF)** that bridges the gap. The C# custom action project template that's installed in Visual Studio with the WiX toolset starts out with a reference to the `Microsoft.Deployment.WindowsInstaller` assembly. That's DTF.

The convention is to have a data-driven approach to custom actions. During the installation sequence (or the immediate phase of the execute sequence), you can collect information and set properties with it. Then, during the deferred phase of the execute sequence, use the information in those properties to makes system changes. In this recipe, we will set the value of a WiX property from within a C# custom action with the convention of collecting information during the UI phase, and using it during the deferred portion of the execute sequence.

In this recipe, we use C# to find the computer's time zone. This is great for demonstration purposes but know that the same information can also be found in the Windows registry under `HKEY_LOCAL_MACHINE\SYSTEM\CurrentControlSet\Control\TimeZoneInformation`.

Getting ready

To prepare for this recipe, create a new setup project and call it `CustomActionInstaller`.

How to do it...

Use the C# custom action project template in Visual Studio to set up the skeleton of the custom action and then add your task-specific code. After compiling, reference the unmanaged version of the assembly—the one with CA in its name—in your setup project using a `Binary` element. Use the `CustomAction` element to include the C# custom action in the installer, and then schedule it into the installer sequence:

1. Add a custom action project by right-clicking on the solution in **Solution Explorer** and going to **Add | New Project... | C# Custom Action Project**. Name it `TimeZoneCustomAction`. Before clicking on **OK** to create the project, pay attention to the version of the .NET Framework listed in the drop-down menu at the top of the dialog. Users will need to have that version of .NET installed to run our custom action, so use the lowest version you can get away with. For this example, .NET 2.0 is enough to go on. Have a look at the following screenshot:

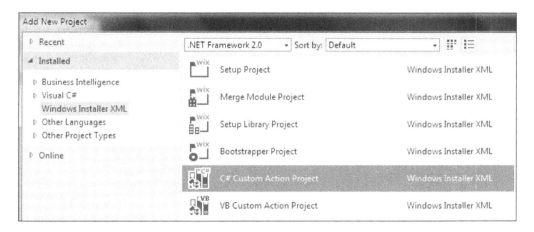

2. Open `CustomAction.cs` and add the following code to it:

```
using Microsoft.Deployment.WindowsInstaller;
using System;

namespace TimeZoneCustomAction
{
  public class CustomActions
  {
    [CustomAction]
    public static ActionResult GetTimeZone(Session session)
    {
      string timeZoneName =
        TimeZone.CurrentTimeZone.StandardName;

      // store the time zone in a property
      session["TIME_ZONE"] = timeZoneName;

      return ActionResult.Success;
    }
  }
}
```

3. Add the custom action to the installer by right-clicking on the **References** node in the setup project and going to **Add Reference... | Projects | TimeZoneCustomAction | Add | OK**.

4. When we compile our custom action project, we'll get two DLLs as the output. The first is a regular managed DLL that the Windows installer can't use. The second, which will append a CA to the name of the DLL, is an unmanaged dynamic-link library that wraps our C# code. We only need to reference the second one in our installer. In `Product.wxs`, inside the `Product` element, add a `Binary` element that has a `SourceFile` attribute pointing to `TimeZoneCustomAction.CA.dll`:

```
<Binary Id="TimeZoneCustomActionDLL"    SourceFile="$(var.
TimeZoneCustomAction.TargetDir)TimeZoneCustomAction.CA.dll" />
```

5. Beneath that, add a `CustomAction` element that points to our C# custom action method. Reference the `Binary` element with the `BinaryKey` attribute:

```
<CustomAction Id="CA_GetTimeZone"
              BinaryKey="TimeZoneCustomActionDLL"
              DllEntry="GetTimeZone"
              Execute="immediate"
              Return="check" />
```

6. To schedule the action during the UI sequence, add a `Custom` element inside an `InstallUISequence` element. Use the `Custom` element's `Before` and `After` attributes to schedule it in relation to the other existing actions:

```
<InstallUISequence>
  <Custom Action="CA_GetTimeZone" After="LaunchConditions" />
</InstallUISequence>
```

7. In order to see that our custom action has run successfully, launch the compiled installer from the command line with the flag `/l*v install.log`. This will create a log that you can read through to see if our `TIME_ZONE` property was set:

msiexec /i CustomActionInstaller.msi /l*v install.log

8. Open `install.log` and verify that the `TIME_ZONE` property was set:

MSI (c) (4C!44) [15:56:03:109]: PROPERTY CHANGE: Adding TIME_ZONE property. Its value is 'Eastern Standard Time'.

 The installer that we've created in this recipe won't actually be installed if you run it because we didn't include any files to be installed. However, you should still be able to run it and get a log of the installation.

How it works...

WiX makes it easy to create a C# custom action because there's a project template for it in Visual Studio. Our C# file uses the `Microsoft.Deployment.WindowsInstaller` namespace to hook on to the installer process and grab the `session` object. The `session` object is what allows us to read and write to WiX properties. In this case, we're setting a property called `TIME_ZONE` by using the indexer on the `session` object.

```
session["TIME_ZONE"] = timeZoneName;
```

If a property with that name doesn't exist, it will be created. Otherwise, it will overwrite the existing property.

Our custom action method must return an object of type `ActionResult`. This can be set to either `ActionResult.Success` or `ActionResult.Failure` to let the installer know whether things went smoothly during the execution of the C# code. For us, since there's no chance of encountering a problem while reading the `TimeZone.CurrentTimeZone.StandardName` property, we simply return `ActionResult.Success`:

```
return ActionResult.Success;
```

We can wrap riskier code in a `try...catch` block to trap exceptions and then return `ActionResult.Failure`. Alternatively, we can allow exceptions to bubble up to the installer. Either way, it will trigger a rollback to undo all of the work up to that point and then quit the installation. Which method you choose will probably depend on how descriptive the exception messages are and whether you'd be better off writing the details of the error to the log yourself. You can call `session.Log()` to write messages to the install log throughout the processing of your method.

Note that only the deferred phase of the execute sequence has rollback capabilities. The UI sequence and the immediate phase of the execute sequence do not. That's okay because we shouldn't be making any changes to the computer during those parts of the installation. Our example, which only sets a property, is fine to run during the UI sequence.

To use this custom action, we referenced the `TimeZoneCustomAction` project and then added a `Binary` element that points to the compiled `TimeZoneCustomAction.CA.dll`. In order to invoke a specific method from that assembly, we added a `CustomAction` element whose `BinaryKey` points to the `Binary` element we just created. Its `DllEntry` attribute identifies the method to call, as follows:

```
<Binary Id="TimeZoneCustomActionDLL"              SourceFile="$(var.
TimeZoneCustomAction.TargetDir)TimeZoneCustomAction.CA.dll" />

<CustomAction Id="CA_GetTimeZone"
              BinaryKey="TimeZoneCustomActionDLL"
              DllEntry="GetTimeZone"
              Execute="immediate"
              Return="check" />
```

We set the `CustomAction` element's `Return` attribute to ensure that our `Success/Failure` status will be reviewed by the installer. In some cases, such as custom actions that run during uninstallation—at which point you probably wouldn't want to prevent the user from removing the software—you can set `Return` to ignore.

We set the `CustomAction` element's `Execute` attribute to `immediate`, which means that the action will be called outside the rollback protected transaction that's used by our installer. For custom actions that change the user's system, we should set `Execute` to `deferred` and schedule it during `InstallExecuteSequence` somewhere between the `InstallInitialize` and `InstallFinalize` actions. However, our `GetTimeZone` custom action is scheduled during `InstallUISequence`:

```
<InstallUISequence>
  <Custom Action="CA_GetTimeZone" After="LaunchConditions" />
</InstallUISequence>
```

The `InstallUISequence` element coincides when the GUI is shown. The `Custom` element references our `CustomAction` element. It allows us to say where within `InstallUISequence` we'd like our action to run. For this example, I put it right after the `LaunchConditions` action. That's pretty much near the start of the installation process. Use the `Orca.exe` file to open your MSI file and see the order of the actions in the `InstallUISequence` and `InstallExecuteSequence` tables:

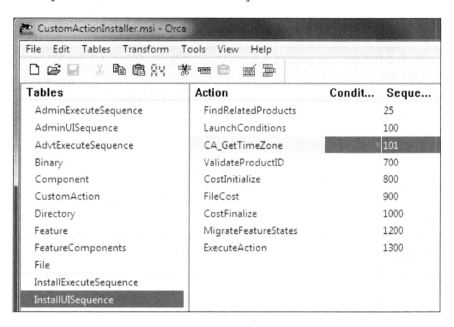

For other custom actions you make, refer to the following website for information about different actions that already exist in the installer so that you can schedule yours appropriately around them:

`http://msdn.microsoft.com/en-us/library/aa372023(v=vs.85).aspx`

For example, if your action depends on files already being copied to the end user's computer, you might want to schedule it after the `InstallFiles` action in `InstallExecuteSequence`. Once you've set up your first custom action, you can schedule additional ones around it, as follows:

```
<InstallUISequence>
  <Custom Action="CA_GetTimeZone" After="LaunchConditions" />
  <Custom Action="CA_AnotherOne" After="CA_GetTimeZone" />
</InstallUISequence>
```

There's more...

Often, you'll only want to invoke a custom action under specific circumstances. For example, you might only want it to run during installation and not during uninstallation. To accomplish this, we can add a conditional statement inside the Custom element. The following example tells the installer only to invoke the custom action if we're performing an initial installation:

```
<Custom Action="CA_AnInstallOnlyMethod"
        After="InstallInitialize">
  <![CDATA[NOT Installed]]>
</Custom>
```

The NOT Installed statement is only true during an installation. We can schedule an action to run only during uninstallation by using the REMOVE ~= "ALL" statement. The following code snippet illustrates this:

```
<Custom Action="CA_AnUninstallMethod"
        After="InstallInitialize">
  <![CDATA[REMOVE ~= "ALL"]]>
</Custom>
```

Passing information entered by a user to a deferred custom action

When the end user provides information to the installer, either through a user interface or the command line, we typically store it in WiX properties so that it can be used later during InstallExecuteSequence. However, we cannot pass these properties directly to a custom action that is scheduled as deferred during InstallExecuteSequence. If you try, you'll get the following error in the install log:

```
Microsoft.Deployment.WindowsInstaller.InstallerException: Cannot
access session details from a non-immediate custom action
```

This is because deferred actions have a heightened level of security and only allow a few properties to be accessed. In this recipe, we will discuss a way to pass our own properties to a deferred custom action.

Getting ready

To prepare for this recipe, perform the following steps:

1. Create a new setup project and name it `PassingPropertyInstaller`.

2. Add a text file to the project called `Sample.txt` and include it in the installer by using the `Component` and `File` elements. The reason we're doing this is so that when we try passing a property to a deferred custom action without using the steps in this recipe, we'll see the error that occurs. If we don't install any files, we'll get a different error for not installing any files. Use the following markup to include a file in the installer:

```
<ComponentGroup Id="ProductComponents"
                Directory="INSTALLFOLDER">
  <Component Id="cmpSampleTXT"
             Guid="{D362EAE1-1219-4E4D-AD5D-048DAB82CAFE}">
    <File Source="Sample.txt" />
  </Component>
</ComponentGroup>
```

3. Add a C# custom action project named `ReadPropertyCustomAction` to the same Visual Studio solution and save the following code to its `CustomAction.cs` file:

```csharp
using Microsoft.Deployment.WindowsInstaller;

namespace ReadPropertyCustomAction
{
  public class CustomActions
  {
    [CustomAction]
    public static ActionResult ReadProperty(Session session)
    {
      // Try to read a property called USERNAME.
      // This will fail!
      string userName = session["USERNAME"];
      session.Log("Username is " + userName);

      return ActionResult.Success;
    }
  }
}
```

4. Reference this project in your setup project and then add the `Binary` and `CustomAction` elements to it, making sure to set the `CustomAction` element's `Execute` attribute to `deferred`:

```
<Binary Id="ReadPropertyCustomActionDLL"
SourceFile="$(var.ReadPropertyCustomAction.TargetDir)
ReadPropertyCustomAction.CA.dll" />


<CustomAction Id="CA_ReadProperty"
              BinaryKey="ReadPropertyCustomActionDLL"
              DllEntry="ReadProperty"
              Execute="deferred"
              Return="check" />
```

5. Schedule the custom action during `InstallExecuteSequence`, after the `InstallInitialize` action, as follows:

```
<InstallExecuteSequence>
  <Custom Action="CA_ReadProperty"
          After="InstallInitialize" />
</InstallExecuteSequence>
```

6. When our deferred custom action is invoked during `InstallExecuteSequence`, it will attempt to read a property called USERNAME. The last thing to do is add a `Property` element that sets USERNAME to a value. In a more real-world scenario, it will be set by the user through the GUI or command line. Use the following code to set the property:

```
<Property Id="USERNAME" Value="joe" />
```

7. After compiling the project, open a command prompt and run the installer with logging turned on. You should see the exception, `Cannot access details from a non-immediate custom action`, in the log. You can use the following command to get an install log:

```
msiexec /i PassingPropertyInstaller.msi /l*v install.txt
```

How to do it...

Use the `SetProperty` element to set a property that has the same ID as our deferred `CustomAction` element. Its `Value` attribute should include the property that we want to pass. The deferred custom action method will then be able to access USERNAME through the session object's `CustomActionData` property. Follow the given steps to pass information entered by a user to a deferred custom action:

1. Add a `SetProperty` element that has the same `ID` as our `CustomAction` element, which in this case is `CA_ReadProperty`. Set its `Value` attribute to our `USERNAME` property in the form `propertyname=[propertyname]`:

```
<SetProperty Id="CA_ReadProperty"
             Value="USERNAME=[USERNAME]"
             Sequence="execute"
             Before="CA_ReadProperty" />
```

2. Within our C# custom action, remove the following line:

```
string userName = session["USERNAME"];
```

3. Replace it with the following code wherein we use `CustomActionData` to access the `USERNAME` property:

```
string userName = session.CustomActionData["USERNAME"];
```

4. In order to see that our custom action has run successfully, launch the compiled installer from the command line with logging turned on. Review the log and verify that the message `Username is Joe` is there. You can use the following command to make a log of the installation:

```
msiexec /i PassingPropertyInstaller.msi /l*v install.log
```

How it works...

At first, we tried to access a property in a deferred custom action using the indexer on the `session` object:

```
string userName = session["USERNAME"];
```

This fails because a property that is set with a `Property` element or set during the immediate phase of the UI or execute sequence, will exist in a completely different context than a deferred custom action within the execute sequence. Passing a property to that type of custom action takes a little extra effort. If we're following the data-driven approach of collecting information from the user through the GUI and then acting upon it during the deferred stage of the execute sequence, then we'll run into this quite often.

In this recipe, we used the `SetProperty` element to create a new property during installation that has the same ID as our deferred custom action. This is how data is put into `CustomActionData` of a custom action. By using the `key=[value]` syntax for the `Value` attribute, we're able to use `CustomActionData` like a hash:

```
string userName = session.CustomActionData["USERNAME"];
```

When we use `SetProperty`, behind the scenes it creates a custom action for us—a Type 51 custom action—that sets up `CustomActionData` for us. This `SetProperty` element must be scheduled to run before our deferred custom action does. Use its `Sequence` attribute to put it into the execute sequence and its `Before` attribute to place it before our deferred custom action.

We may also pass more than one value by separating them with semicolons, as in the following example:

```
<SetProperty Id="CA_ReadProperty"
            Value="USERNAME=[USERNAME];PASSWORD=[PASSWORD]"
            Sequence="execute"
            Before="CA_ReadProperty" />
```

Then, in our custom action, access each property, as follows:

```
string userName = session.CustomActionData["USERNAME"];
string password = session.CustomActionData["PASSWORD"];
```

Preventing custom action data from being displayed in the install log

When you install an MSI file with logging turned on, the `Property` elements that you've set will be displayed in the log. To make things more secure, the first thing we should do is add the `Hidden` attribute to each `Property` element that contains private information. For example, say we had a property called `PASSWORD` and we set its `Hidden` attribute to `yes`, as follows:

```
<Property Id="PASSWORD"
          Value="my_password"
          Hidden="yes" />
```

Now, the value of that property will be replaced with asterisks in the log:

```
Property(S): PASSWORD = **********
```

Unfortunately, if we pass that same property to a deferred custom action using the `CustomActionData` technique shown in the previous recipe, such as the following:

```
<SetProperty Id="CA_ReadProperty"
            Value="PASSWORD=[PASSWORD]"
            Sequence="execute"
            Before="CA_ReadProperty" />
```

Then the PASSWORD value will be visible. Here's a sample of what will be shown in the log after the SetCA_ReadProperty custom action, which is created behind the scenes when the SetProperty element is invoked:

```
Action start 22:17:53: SetCA_ReadProperty.
MSI (s) (B0:78) [22:17:53:316]: PROPERTY CHANGE: Adding CA_
ReadProperty property. Its value is 'PASSWORD=my_password'.
```

In this recipe, we will see how to prevent CustomActionData from displaying in the install log.

Getting ready

To prepare for this recipe, perform the following steps:

1. Create a new setup project and call it HidingLogDataInstaller.

2. Add a text file called Sample.txt to the project and include it in the installer by using the Component and File elements. If we don't install any files, we'll get an error. Use the following markup to include the file in the installer:

```
<ComponentGroup Id="ProductComponents"
                Directory="INSTALLFOLDER">
  <Component Id="cmpSampleTXT"
             Guid="{D362EAE1-1219-4E4D-AD5D-048DAB82CAFE}">
    <File Source="Sample.txt" />
  </Component>
</ComponentGroup>
```

3. Include a C# custom action project in the same Visual Studio solution and call it ReadPropertyCustomAction. Update its CustomAction.cs file with the following code:

```
using Microsoft.Deployment.WindowsInstaller;

namespace ReadPropertyCustomAction
{
  public class CustomActions
  {
    [CustomAction]
    public static ActionResult ReadProperty(Session session)
    {
      string passworduserName =
        session.CustomActionData["PASSWORD"];

      return ActionResult.Success;
    }
  }
}
```

4. Reference this project in your setup project and include it using the `Binary` and `CustomAction` elements:

```
<Binary Id="ReadPropertyCustomActionDLL" SourceFile="$(var.
ReadPropertyCustomAction.TargetDir)ReadPropertyCustomAction.
CA.dll" />

<CustomAction Id="CA_ReadProperty"
              BinaryKey="ReadPropertyCustomActionDLL"
              DllEntry="ReadProperty"
              Execute="deferred"
              Return="check" />
```

5. Include the custom action in `InstallExecuteSequence`:

```
<InstallExecuteSequence>
  <Custom Action="CA_ReadProperty"
        After="InstallInitialize" />
</InstallExecuteSequence>
```

6. Add a `Property` element with ID as `PASSWORD` and assign it a value. Set its `Hidden` attribute to `yes`:

```
<Property Id="PASSWORD"
          Value="my_password"
          Hidden="yes" />
```

7. Add a `SetProperty` element to create `CustomActionData` for our deferred custom action:

```
<SetProperty Id="CA_ReadProperty"
             Value="PASSWORD=[PASSWORD]"
             Sequence="execute"
             Before="CA_ReadProperty" />
```

8. Now, if we were to run this installer, we'd see the `PASSWORD` property exposed in the log. We're ready to see how to hide that information.

How to do it...

Add the `HideTarget` attribute to the `CustomAction` element so that any data that's sent to it will be hidden. The following steps will show you how.

1. Locate the `CustomAction` element of the deferred custom action and set its `HideTarget` attribute to `yes`:

```
<CustomAction Id="CA_ReadProperty"
              BinaryKey="ReadPropertyCustomActionDLL"
              DllEntry="ReadProperty"
```

```
Execute="deferred"
Return="check"
HideTarget="yes"/>
```

2. To verify that the property has been hidden in the log, run the installer from the command line with logging turned on. Use the following command:

    ```
    msiexec /i HidingLogDataInstaller.msi /l*v install.log
    ```

How it works...

When you want to hide the value of a `Property` element that's passed to a deferred custom action, add the `HideTarget` attribute to the `CustomAction` element itself. Any data that's sent to that custom action will be hidden. Everywhere that the `PASSWORD` value is shown in the log will now show only asterisks. Here's a sample of the updated log:

```
Action start 23:02:45: SetCA_ReadProperty.
```
```
MSI (s) (B0:94) [23:02:45:477]: PROPERTY CHANGE: Adding CA_ReadProperty
property. Its value is '**********'.
```

Running an executable as a custom action without showing a console window by using CAQuietExec

As you may know, it's possible to execute a Windows batch script as a custom action. Then again, if you're able to not use a batch script, preferring a more robust mechanism such as a C# custom action, then that's better. However, sometimes you just can't avoid it. In those cases, one annoyance is that a console window will be displayed while the batch script is running. In this recipe, we'll see how to hide it from the user.

Getting ready

To prepare for this recipe, perform the following steps:

1. Create a new setup project and call it `QuietCustomActionInstaller`.
2. We will create a batch script that prints a sequence of numbers to the console for a few seconds, long enough to be noticeable. Open a text editor such as notepad and enter the following code:

    ```
    @ECHO OFF
    FOR /L %%i IN (1,1,10000) DO ECHO %%i
    ```

3. Save this file as `BatchScript.cmd` and put it in the same folder as your setup project.

4. Reference it in your project by right-clicking on the `QuietCustomActionInstaller` project in **Solution Explorer** and going to **Add | Existing Item...**. Then, on the **Add Existing Item** window, change the file type selection box to display all files and select the `BatchScript.cmd` file. Click on the **Add** button.

5. Include the batch script in the installer by adding the `Component` and `File` elements that point to it. Be sure to give the `File` element an `Id` attribute so that we can reference this particular `File` element later:

```
<ComponentGroup Id="ProductComponents"
                Directory="INSTALLFOLDER">
  <Component Id="cmpBatchScriptCMD"
             Guid="{14EF1451-3726-4598-A1FC-7E6556900340}">
    <File Id="fileBatchScriptCMD"
          Source="BatchScript.cmd" />
  </Component>
</ComponentGroup>
```

 The reason I suggest using Notepad or a similar program to create the batch file is that Visual Studio will often insert invisible unicode characters into the file that will prevent the script from running correctly. Once created by another editor, it's fine to add it to the project and work with it from within Visual Studio.

How to do it...

Use the `CAQuietExec` custom action from `UtilExtension` to hide the console window of a batch script that's executed during the installation:

1. Add `UtilExtension` to the project by right-clicking on the `References` node in **Solution Explorer** and navigating to **Add Reference... | WixUtilExtension.dll | Add | OK**.

2. Add a `CustomAction` element that has its `BinaryKey` attribute set to `WixCA`, its `DllEntry` attribute set to `CAQuietExec`, and its `Execute` attribute set to `deferred`:

```
<CustomAction Id="CA_RunBatchScript"
              BinaryKey="WixCA"
              DllEntry="CAQuietExec"
              Execute="deferred"
              Return="check" />
```

3. Schedule the custom action to run during `InstallExecuteSequence` after the `InstallFiles` action:

```
<InstallExecuteSequence>
  <Custom Action="CA_RunBatchScript" After="InstallFiles" />
</InstallExecuteSequence>
```

4. Use a `SetProperty` element to create `CustomActionData` for the `CA_RunBatchScript` custom action. Its `Value` attribute will be the command we'd like to run. The following snippet uses the ID of our batch script's `File` element to get the full path to the file after it's been installed. We surround it with `&quot;` entities so that the path will have quotes around it, if it contains spaces:

```
<SetProperty Id="CA_RunBatchScript"
             Value="&quot;[#fileBatchScriptCMD]&quot;"
             Sequence="execute"
             Before="CA_RunBatchScript" />
```

How it works...

We added our `BatchScript.cmd` file to the installer using the `Component` and `File` elements. This installs it to the end user's computer so that we can execute it as part of our installation. Note that we set the `CustomAction` element's `BinaryKey` to `WixCA` and its `DllEntry` to `CAQuietExec` in order to invoke our script silently. The `CAQuietExec` action, which is included in the WiX `UtilExtension` namespace, runs our commands for us. Since, in most cases, running a batch script is meant to change the state of the end user's computer, we set the custom action to run as deferred during `InstallExecuteSequence`.

To instruct the `CAQuietExec` custom action which commands to run, we must pass them via `CustomActionData`. So, we added a `SetProperty` element to do just that, setting its `Value` attribute to the ID of our batch script's `File` element preceded by a hash sign. During installation, this placeholder will be replaced by the full path to our `BatchScript.cmd` file. When the script is executed, the end user won't see its console window at all. Behind the scenes, the `CAQuietExec` action launches the batch script in a process that has the `CREATE_NO_WINDOW` process creation flag.

There's more...

If you need to pass arguments to your batch script, you can pass them as part of the formatted string you assign to the `SetProperty` element's `Value` attribute, for example, suppose you wanted to pass an IP address to the script. If the IP address is stored in a property, it can be referenced by surrounding it with square brackets, as follows:

```
<Property Id="IPADDRESS" Value="127.0.0.1" />

<SetProperty
```

```
      Id="CA_RunBatchScript"
      Value="&quot;[#fileBatchScriptCMD]&quot; [IPADDRESS]"
      Sequence="execute"
      Before="CA_RunBatchScript" />
```

Try it out by reading the argument within the batch script and printing it to the console. Use the following code:

```
@ECHO OFF
SET IP_ADDRESS=%1
FOR /L %%i IN (1,1,10000) DO ECHO %%i - %IP_ADDRESS%
```

Now, the IP address will be included on each line that's printed to the console window. You can run the installer with logging turned on to see this, since you won't actually see any console window:

```
msiexec /i QuietCustomActionInstaller.msi /l*v install.log
```

Testing rollback custom actions with WixFailWhenDeferred

For every custom action that changes the end user's system, you should also author a rollback custom action that reverts those changes in the event of an error. The big question then is how do we test that the rollback works? In this recipe, we'll briefly outline a scenario where a rollback will be needed and then discuss how to trigger one for testing purposes.

In our example, there will be a file that already exists on the computer. Our installer updates a value within it. However, if the installation fails for some reason and a rollback is triggered, the file should be reverted to its original state.

Getting ready

To prepare for this recipe, perform the following steps:

1. On the computer where you'll be running the installer, add a file called Config.js. Place it in the target machine's C: drive so that it's at C:\Config.js. Our installer will update this file, but revert it to its original version if there's an error during installation. Add the following to the file:

   ```
   {
      "serverAddress" : "127.0.0.1"
   }
   ```

2. Create a new setup project called RollbackTestingInstaller.

3. Add the following markup, which will find the `Config.js` file on the `C:` drive and store its full path in a WiX property called `FILE_PATH`:

```
<Property Id="FILE_PATH">
  <DirectorySearch Id="CDriveSearch"
                   Path="[WindowsVolume]"
                   Depth="0"
                   AssignToProperty="no">
    <FileSearch Id="ConfigJsSearch" Name="Config.js" />
  </DirectorySearch>
</Property>
```

4. Add a text file to the project called `Sample.txt` and include it in the installer by using the `Component` and `File` elements. If we don't install any files, we'll get an error for not installing any files. Use the following markup to include a file in the installer:

```
<ComponentGroup Id="ProductComponents"
                Directory="INSTALLFOLDER">
  <Component Id="cmpSampleTXT"
             Guid="{01AFDE2B-0A59-43D6-82B2-3A07998E08B7}">
    <File Source="Sample.txt" />
  </Component>
</ComponentGroup>
```

5. Add a C# custom action project to the same Visual Studio solution and call it `FileChangingCustomActions`.

6. We are going to define three methods in the `CustomActions.cs` file. The first method we'll call is `StoreExistingFile`. It will open the `Config.js` file that already exists on the end user's computer and store the contents of that file in `CustomActionData`, which we'll pass to our rollback custom action. This way, if a rollback occurs, it will have the file's original contents to revert back to. Like deferred actions, rollback actions can only read WiX properties that are passed via `CustomActionData`. However, as you can see, we can set `CustomActionData` from within an immediate custom action, such as our `StoreExistingFile` method. Update `CustomActions.cs` with the following code:

```
using Microsoft.Deployment.WindowsInstaller;
using System;
using System.IO;

namespace FileChangingCustomActions
{
  public class CustomActions
  {
    [CustomAction]
```

```
      public static ActionResult StoreExistingFile(
        Session session)
      {
        string filePath = session["FILE_PATH"];

        if (File.Exists(filePath))
        {
          string content = File.ReadAllText(filePath);

          // Set CustomActionData for rollback method
          CustomActionData data = new CustomActionData();
          data["FILE_CONTENT"] = content;
          data["FILE_PATH"] = filePath;
          session["CA_RollbackFile"] = data.ToString();
        }
        else
        {
          session.Log("File not found: " + filePath);
          return ActionResult.Failure;
        }

        return ActionResult.Success;
      }
    }
  }
```

7. Next, define the `ChangeFile` custom action. This is the method that updates the `Config.js` file as part of the normal installation. Add the following method to our `CustomActions.cs` file:

```
[CustomAction]
public static ActionResult ChangeFile(Session session)
{
  string filePath = session.CustomActionData["FILE_PATH"];

  if (File.Exists(filePath))
  {
    string originalContent = File.ReadAllText(filePath);
    string updatedContent =
      originalContent.Replace(
        "\"serverAddress\" : \"127.0.0.1\"",
        "\"serverAddress\" : \"10.0.0.1\"");

    File.WriteAllText(filePath, updatedContent);
  }

  return ActionResult.Success;
}
```

8. Then, define the custom action that will undo these changes in the event of a rollback. We can call it `RollbackFile`. Add the following method to `CustomActions.cs`:

```
[CustomAction]
public static ActionResult RollbackFile(Session session)
{
  string filePath = session.CustomActionData["FILE_PATH"];

  if (File.Exists(filePath))
  {
    string originalContent =
      session.CustomActionData["FILE_CONTENT"];

    File.WriteAllText(filePath, originalContent);
  }

  return ActionResult.Success;
}
```

9. Reference the custom action project in your setup project and then add a `Binary` element for it:

```
<Binary Id="FileChangingCustomActionsDLL" SourceFile="$(var.
FileChangingCustomActions.TargetDir)FileChangingCustomActions.
CA.dll" />
```

10. Include the custom actions in the installer using the `CustomAction` elements. Note the `Execute` attribute of each element and also that we're ignoring the `Return` value of the rollback custom action so that if it fails, it won't prevent the rest of the software from being rolled back:

```
<CustomAction Id="CA_StoreExistingFile"
              BinaryKey="FileChangingCustomActionsDLL"
              DllEntry="StoreExistingFile"
              Execute="immediate"
              Return="check" />

<CustomAction Id="CA_ChangeFile"
              BinaryKey="FileChangingCustomActionsDLL"
              DllEntry="ChangeFile"
              Execute="deferred"
              Return="check" />

<CustomAction Id="CA_RollbackFile"
              BinaryKey="FileChangingCustomActionsDLL"
              DllEntry="RollbackFile"
              Execute="rollback"
              Return="ignore" />
```

11. Add the actions to the execute sequence and order them so that
    `StoreExistingFile` is executed first, then `RollbackFile`,
    and then `ChangeFile`, as follows:

```
<InstallExecuteSequence>
  <Custom Action="CA_StoreExistingFile"
          Before="InstallFinalize">
    <![CDATA[NOT Installed]]>
  </Custom>

  <Custom Action="CA_RollbackFile"
          After="CA_StoreExistingFile">
    <![CDATA[NOT Installed]]>
  </Custom>

  <Custom Action="CA_ChangeFile"
          After="CA_RollbackFile">
    <![CDATA[NOT Installed]]>
  </Custom>
</InstallExecuteSequence>
```

12. The `ChangeFile` method needs the path to the file. We can set
    `CustomActionData` with a `SetProperty` element, as follows:

```
<SetProperty Id="CA_ChangeFile"
             Value="FILE_PATH=[FILE_PATH]"
             Sequence="execute"
             Before="CA_ChangeFile" />
```

13. If you compile and run the installer, it should find the `Config.js` file on the desktop
    and update it so that it contains 10.0.0.1 instead of 127.0.0.1. However, we want to
    test what would happen if a rollback were to occur. This recipe will show you how to
    simulate one.

How to do it...

Use the `WixFailWhenDeferred` custom action from `UtilExtension` to manually invoke a
rollback, so that we can verify that our rollback custom action is working correctly:

1. Add `UtilExtension` to the project by right-clicking on the `References` node in
   Solution Explorer and going to **Add Reference... | WixUtilExtension.dll | Add | OK**.

2. Add a `CustomActionRef` element that has an `Id` attribute of
   `WixFailWhenDeferred`. This can go inside your `Product` element after the
   `Package` element:

```
<CustomActionRef Id="WixFailWhenDeferred" />
```

3. Run the installer from the command line but this time, pass WIXFAILWHENDEFERRED=1 to it so that a rollback is triggered towards the end of the installation:

```
msiexec /i RollbackTestingInstaller.msi WIXFAILWHENDEFERRED=1
```

4. The installation should fail and roll back. Check our Config.js file to make sure that it has kept its original contents. It should contain 127.0.0.1 and not 10.0.0.1.

How it works...

The UtilExtension namespace contains a custom action called WixFailWhenDeferred, which, when added to a project, will schedule itself within the execute sequence so that right at the end, a rollback is triggered. However, you control whether to invoke the rollback by passing WIXFAILWHENDEFERRED=1 on the command line; otherwise, it will continue without a rollback.

It's a good idea to always include WixFailWhenDeferred in your setup projects. This way, you always have a way to test a rollback. This sort of testing, along with verifying that uninstallation works correctly, is an important part of assuring the quality of your installer.

7
Installing Wizards

In this chapter, we will cover the following:

- ▶ Adding a wizard to guide users through the installation
- ▶ Changing the logo images and default license agreement text of the wizard
- ▶ Customizing the wizard by adding a new dialog window to it
- ▶ Deciding which dialog to show next depending on the user's choices
- ▶ Setting a property based on user input

Introduction

Before you add your own user interface, your MSI will give the minimum amount of feedback during the installation. There will be a progress bar and a cancel button, but that's about it. The user won't get any lead-up before their computer is suddenly being altered. This can be pretty unnerving for the end user.

The good news is that we can add a UI using the same declarative XML syntax that we've used in the rest of our setup project. Even better, the WiX toolset ships with several ready-made install wizards that we can use as is or customize. A user interface doesn't have to mean slowing down unattended, automated installs either. We can turn our UI off by running the MSI from the command line with the `/quiet` flag, as follows:

```
msiexec /i MyInstaller.msi /quiet
```

In this chapter, we'll get familiar with using the WiX toolset's wizards and how to customize them. We'll also see how to save the choices the user has made through the UI so that we can use that information in later parts of the install.

Adding a wizard to guide users through the installation

`UIExtension` is where we can find several premade user interfaces to guide users through the installation. Here are five premade user interfaces: `WixUI_Advanced`, `WixUI_FeatureTree`, `WixUI_InstallDir`, `WixUI_Mondo`, and `WixUI_Minimal`. Each has some unique features. For example, `WixUI_InstallDir` lets you change the target install directory and `WixUI_Mondo` gives users the option to install a typical, custom, or complete setup. `WixUI_Minimal` is the easiest to get started with, since it only has one dialog. In this recipe, we'll add it to our setup project to give you a feel of how it works.

Getting ready

To prepare for this recipe, perform the following steps:

1. Create a new setup project and call it `InstallerWithWizard`.

2. For the installer to complete successfully, you should add at least one file to it. Add a file called `Sample.txt` and then include a `Component` and `File` element for it:

```
<ComponentGroup Id="ProductComponents"
                Directory="INSTALLFOLDER">
  <Component Id="cmpSampleTXT"
             Guid="{2D1D0EC9-7DD9-4948-A175-59C9B2001B12}">
    <File Source="Sample.txt" />
  </Component>
</ComponentGroup>
```

How to do it...

Add a `UIRef` element that points to one of the user interfaces that's defined in `UIExtension` to display the UI during the installation. The following steps will show you how:

1. Add the `UIExtension` namespace to the project by right-clicking on the `References` node in **Solution Explorer** and navigating to **Add Reference...** | **WixUIExtension.dll** | **Add** | **OK**.

2. Add a `UIRef` element, either inside the `Product` element after the `Package` element or within its own fragment, with `Id` set to `WixUI_Minimal`. Here's an example:

```
<UIRef Id="WixUI_Minimal"/>
```

3. Compile and run the installer to see the new user interface.

How it works...

The `UIExtension` contains the markup that defines the layout of several user interfaces. The only thing you need to do is reference the one you want. If you were to look at the source code of UIExtension, you'd see that it uses a `UI` element as the parent container that assembles all the buttons, checkboxes, and text on each dialog. A `UIRef` element makes an association with that `UI` element and pulls in all of its content. Its `Id` attribute matches `Id` on the `UI` element.

There's more...

Some of these install wizards require extra setup, such as setting properties that will be displayed in the UI. `WixUI_Advanced` needs you to give your installation's top-level `Directory` element an ID of `APPLICATIONFOLDER`, as shown:

```
<Directory Id="TARGETDIR" Name="SourceDir">
  <Directory Id="ProgramFilesFolder">
    <Directory Id="APPLICATIONFOLDER" Name="My Company" />
  </Directory>
</Directory>
```

You must also add two properties called `ApplicationFolderName` and `WixAppFolder`. The first should be the name of the folder where our software is installed, as it will be displayed to the end user. The second can be set to either `WixPerMachineFolder` or `WixPerUserFolder` to control whether to default to an installation for all users or only for the current one. The following example sets these two properties:

```
<UIRef Id="WixUI_Advanced"/>
<Property Id="ApplicationFolderName" Value="My Company" />
<Property Id="WixAppFolder" Value="WixPerMachineFolder" />
```

The `WixUI_InstallDir` wizard shows a dialog that lets the user change the install path and expects you to set a property called `WIXUI_INSTALLDIR` to the `Id` of your software's `Directory` element, as follows:

```
<UIRef Id="WixUI_InstallDir"/>
<Property Id="WIXUI_INSTALLDIR" Value="INSTALLFOLDER" />
```

Changing the logo images and default license agreement text of the wizard

When you launch your installer with one of the user interfaces from the WiX Toolset, you'll notice that it has a generic look and defaults to displaying the Common Public License for the EULA. You'll want to customize this to show our own branded images and company-specific license agreement. In this recipe, we will update `WixUI_Minimal` so that it displays a new background and uses the GNU General Public License. This applies to all of the default wizards.

Getting ready

To prepare for this recipe, perform the following steps:

1. Create a new setup project and call it `CustomizedWizardInstaller`.

2. For the installer to complete successfully, you should add at least one file to it. Add a file called `Sample.txt` and then include a `Component` and `File` element in it:

```
<ComponentGroup Id="ProductComponents"
                Directory="INSTALLFOLDER">
  <Component Id="cmpSampleTXT"
             Guid="{A6F5F368-0FD3-4E75-AF3B-9FCB12AD1D86}">
    <File Source="Sample.txt" />
  </Component>
</ComponentGroup>
```

3. Add a reference to the UIExtension namespace and then add a UIRef element that points to WixUI_Minimal:

```
<UIRef Id="WixUI_Minimal"/>
```

How to do it...

Use the WixVariable elements to define image and RTF resources for the user interface:

1. Create a JPEG image that is 493 pixels wide and 312 pixels high. To match how the default image that WiX uses does it, have the left 165 pixels of the background image be a different color. Experiment with colors until you find some that blend well with the checkboxes, labels, and other controls on the dialog:

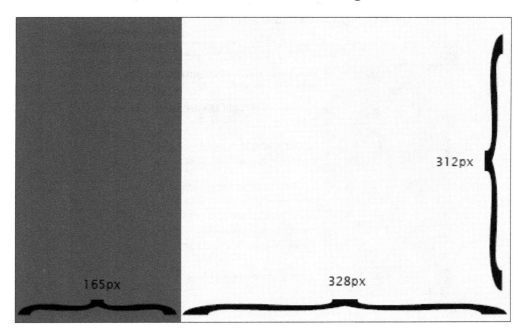

2. Add this image to the setup project. Then, add a WixVariable element that has Id set to WixUIDialogBmp and Value set to your image's path:

```
<UIRef Id="WixUI_Minimal"/>

<WixVariable Id="WixUIDialogBmp"
        Value="CustomBackground.jpg"/>
```

3. To change the license agreement, add your own to a **rich text format** (**RTF**) file using a text editor like Wordpad. Microsoft Word, for some reason, doesn't make RTF files in the correct format. Add this file to the setup project. If the file isn't RTF, or if it isn't formatted correctly, the license won't show up when you run the installer.

4. Add a `WixVariable` element with `Id` of `WixUILicenseRtf` and `Value` that points to the RTF file:

```
<UIRef Id="WixUI_Minimal"/>
<WixVariable Id="WixUIDialogBmp"
             Value="CustomBackground.jpg"/>
<WixVariable Id="WixUILicenseRtf"
             Value="CustomLicense.rtf"/>
```

5. Launch the installer to see the changes to the user interface. Here's an example that uses a GPL and a background with a sidebar of smiley faces:

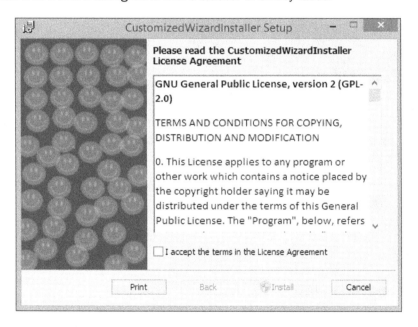

How it works...

The WiX team had customization in mind when they built the wizards that come with the toolset. By simply adding the `WixVariable` elements with the right IDs, we can change the look and content. In this example, we changed the background using a `WixVariable` called `WixUIDialogBmp`, and the license agreement text using a `WixVariable` called `WixUILicenseRtf`.

There's one other image that, although it doesn't make an appearance in the `WixUI_Minimal` wizard, does come into play in the others. It's an image that floats at the top of other dialogs. It has a white background with a red box on its right-hand side that contains a graphic of a CD. Here's the default look for the `WixUI_Mondo` wizard:

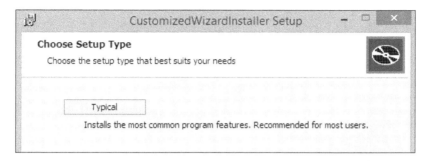

We can change this to another background with dimensions of 493 pixels by 58 pixels using `WixVariable` with `Id` of `WixUIBannerBmp`:

```
<WixVariable Id="WixUIBannerBmp" Value="CustomBanner.jpg"/>
```

Customizing the wizard by adding a new dialog window to it

The wizards that you get with the WiX toolset are great for getting started but probably aren't a perfect fit for the information you hope to collect or display to the user. As you might expect, we can customize them so that they include our own custom screens. For example, if you want to collect a username and password from the user, you can add a screen that asks for this information and stores it in WiX properties.

The `WixUI_Minimal` wizard, which we've used in the previous recipes, has only one screen so it's ill-suited for customization. Let's use `WixUI_InstallDir` instead. It starts out with a license agreement dialog, followed by a dialog that lets the user change the installation directory, and ends with a screen that asks whether they're satisfied with their changes and provides an **Install** button. We will insert a dialog that's mostly blank but includes the **Next**, **Back**, and **Cancel** buttons. You'll be able to use this template for creating any kind of dialog you want.

Getting ready

To prepare for this recipe, perform the following steps:

1. Create a new setup project and call it `NewDialogInstaller`.

2. For the installer to complete successfully, you should add at least one file to it. Add a file called `Sample.txt` and then include a `Component` and `File` element for it:

```
<ComponentGroup Id="ProductComponents"
                Directory="INSTALLFOLDER">
  <Component Id="cmpSampleTXT"
             Guid="{A6F5F368-0FD3-4E75-AF3B-9FCB12AD1D86}">
    <File Source="Sample.txt" />
  </Component>
</ComponentGroup>
```

3. Add a reference to `UIExtension` and add a `UIRef` element that points to `WixUI_InstallDir`:

```
<UIRef Id="WixUI_InstallDir"/>
```

4. This particular wizard requires us to set a property called `WIXUI_INSTALLDIR` so that it matches the `Id` of our software's `Directory` element. Here's an example:

```
<Directory Id="TARGETDIR" Name="SourceDir">
  <Directory Id="ProgramFilesFolder">
    <Directory Id="INSTALLFOLDER" Name="My Company" />
  </Directory>
</Directory>
<Property Id="WIXUI_INSTALLDIR" Value="INSTALLFOLDER" />
```

How to do it...

Override the navigation buttons of an existing user interface so that they take the user to your new dialog. The following steps will show you how:

1. Download the source code for the WiX toolset from `http://wix.codeplex.com/SourceControl/latest`. If you don't want to use the very latest set of code, you can use the dropdown on the page to select your preferred version.

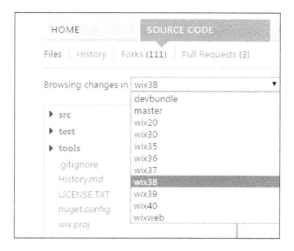

2. Unzip the ZIP file and navigate within it to the `src\ext\UIExtension\wixlib` directory.

3. Find the `.wxs` file that has the same name as the wizard we're using. We're using `WixUI_InstallDir`, so look for `WixUI_InstallDir.wxs`. Copy it to the setup project and rename it to something else, such as `CustomInstallDir.wxs`. You can drag-and-drop files onto Visual Studio's **Solution Explorer** pane to copy them to the project:

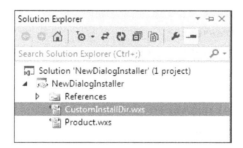

4. Open the new `CustomInstallDir.wxs` file and change its UI element to have `Id` of `CustomInstallDir` instead of `WixUI_InstallDir`:

```
<Wix xmlns="http://schemas.microsoft.com/wix/2006/wi">
    <Fragment>
        <UI Id="CustomInstallDir">
```

5. Within our `Product.wxs` file, update the `UIRef` element that we added earlier so that it points to `CustomInstallDir` instead of `WixUI_InstallDir`:

```
<UIRef Id="CustomInstallDir"/>
```

6. When creating your own dialog, you can reuse the markup from one of the dialogs you got with the WiX source code. Just remove the parts you don't need and add those that you do. Here's a sample based on the `InstallDirDlg.wxs` file that displays a mostly empty dialog with just the **Back**, **Next**, and **Cancel** buttons, and the banner at the top. Save this to the project as `MyCustomDlg.wxs`:

```xml
<?xml version="1.0" encoding="UTF-8"?>
<Wix xmlns="http://schemas.microsoft.com/wix/2006/wi">
<Fragment>
  <UI>
    <Dialog Id="MyCustomDlg"
            Width="370"
            Height="270"
            Title="My Custom Dialog">
      <Control Id="Next"
               Type="PushButton"
               X="236"
               Y="243"
               Width="56"
               Height="17"
               Default="yes"
               Text="!(loc.WixUINext)" />
      <Control Id="Back"
               Type="PushButton"
               X="180"
               Y="243"
               Width="56"
               Height="17"
               Text="!(loc.WixUIBack)" />
      <Control Id="Cancel"
               Type="PushButton"
               X="304"
               Y="243"
               Width="56"
               Height="17"
               Cancel="yes"
               Text="!(loc.WixUICancel)">
        <Publish Event="SpawnDialog"
```

```xml
                        Value="CancelDlg">1</Publish>
        </Control>
        <Control Id="Description"
                Type="Text"
                X="25"
                Y="23"
                Width="280"
                Height="15"
                Transparent="yes"
                NoPrefix="yes"
                Text="My Custom Dialog" />
        <Control Id="Title"
                Type="Text"
                X="15"
                Y="6"
                Width="200"
                Height="15"
                Transparent="yes"
                NoPrefix="yes"
                Text="My Custom Dialog" />
        <Control Id="BannerBitmap"
                Type="Bitmap"
                X="0"
                Y="0"
                Width="370"
                Height="44"
                TabSkip="no"
                Text="!(loc.InstallDirDlgBannerBitmap)" />
        <Control Id="BannerLine"
                Type="Line"
                X="0"
                Y="44"
                Width="370"
                Height="0" />
        <Control Id="BottomLine"
                Type="Line"
```

```
                        X="0"
                        Y="234"
                        Width="370" Height="0" />
        </Dialog>
     </UI>
  </Fragment>
</Wix>
```

7. To insert this new dialog into the existing flow, open `CustomInstallDir.wxs` and update the following lines so that the `InstallDirDlg` dialog's **Next** button and the `VerifyReadyDlg` dialog's **Back** button takes the user to our custom dialog, essentially inserting itself between the two:

```
<Publish Dialog="InstallDirDlg"
         Control="Next"
         Event="NewDialog"
         Value="MyCustomDlg"
         Order="4">
   WIXUI_DONTVALIDATEPATH OR WIXUI_INSTALLDIR_VALID="1"
</Publish>

<Publish Dialog="VerifyReadyDlg"
         Control="Back"
         Event="NewDialog"
         Value="MyCustomDlg"
         Order="1">
   NOT Installed
</Publish>
```

8. Add the following lines so that our own dialog's **Next** and **Back** buttons take the user to the right places:

```
<Publish Dialog="MyCustomDlg"
         Control="Back"
         Event="NewDialog"
         Value="InstallDirDlg" Order="1">1</Publish>

<Publish Dialog="MyCustomDlg"
         Control="Next"
         Event="NewDialog"
         Value="VerifyReadyDlg" Order="1">1</Publish>
```

9. Build the project to verify that our custom dialog now appears as a part of the user interface's sequence of dialogs, as follows:

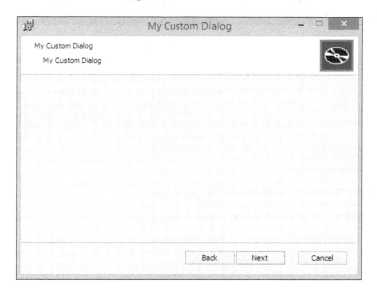

How it works...

When we reference the UIExtension namespace, we get access to several ready-to-go user interfaces. However, we can also add our own master UI that ties together the constituent dialogs in a different way. Then, we just update our UIRef element so that it points to our custom UI element, which mostly reuses dialogs from WixUI_InstallDir.

The WixUI_InstallDir.wxs file is the navigational piece that ties all the dialogs together. We can alter it to control how the screens are sequenced, as well as add our own. The other wizards can be extended in the same way. For example, if we want to customize WixUI_Mondo, we will download the source code and update WixUI_Mondo.wxs. Just remember to rename the file once you've added it to the project.

To insert a new dialog, we updated the Publish elements in WixUI_InstallDir.wxs. The Publish elements control the buttons on each of the dialogs. Specifically, they fire a NewDialog event that causes the screen to transition from one dialog to another. The screen that comes up next is determined by the Publish element's Value attribute. This makes it possible to change the entire wizard's sequence by updating only one file.

Deciding which dialog to show next depending on the user's choices

Sometimes, you'll want to display one dialog or another depending on choices that the user has made up to that point. For example, suppose we ask them whether they want to install a new SQL Server database or use an existing one. Depending on their decision, the next screen they see will either be one that asks for details about the new database or a screen that asks them to specify where the existing database can be found. In this recipe, we'll insert such a dialog and change which dialog to show next depending on the choice the user makes.

Getting ready

To prepare for this recipe, perform the following steps:

1. Create a new setup project and name it `SwitchingDialogsInstaller`.

2. Use the technique discussed in the last recipe, wherein we copy `WixUI_InstallDir.wxs` and rename it `CustomInstallDir.wxs`, to insert a dialog called `DatabaseChoice.wxs` into an existing wizard. This new dialog will be where the user chooses whether they want to create a new database or use an existing one.

3. Add another dialog and call it `NewDatabase.wxs`. It will be used in the event of the user choosing to add a new database. Update its `Dialog` element so that it has `Id` of `NewDatabaseDlg`. Also, change its `Title` control so that it says `New Database Screen`. This way, we know which screen we've landed on. Here's the markup:

```xml
<?xml version="1.0" encoding="UTF-8"?>
<Wix xmlns="http://schemas.microsoft.com/wix/2006/wi">
  <Fragment>
    <UI>
      <Dialog Id="NewDatabaseDlg" Width="370" Height="270"
Title="My Custom Dialog">
        <Control Id="Next" Type="PushButton" X="236" Y="243"
Width="56" Height="17" Default="yes" Text="!(loc.WixUINext)" />
        <Control Id="Back" Type="PushButton" X="180" Y="243"
Width="56" Height="17" Text="!(loc.WixUIBack)" />
        <Control Id="Cancel" Type="PushButton" X="304" Y="243"
Width="56" Height="17" Cancel="yes" Text="!(loc.WixUICancel)">
          <Publish Event="SpawnDialog" Value="CancelDlg">1</
Publish>
        </Control>

        <Control Id="Description" Type="Text" X="25" Y="23"
Width="280" Height="15" Transparent="yes" NoPrefix="yes"
Text="Create a database" />
        <Control Id="Title" Type="Text" X="15" Y="6" Width="200"
Height="15" Transparent="yes" NoPrefix="yes" Text="New Database"
/>
```

```
        <Control Id="BannerBitmap" Type="Bitmap" X="0"
Y="0" Width="370" Height="44" TabSkip="no" Text="!(loc.
InstallDirDlgBannerBitmap)" />
        <Control Id="BannerLine" Type="Line" X="0" Y="44"
Width="370" Height="0" />
        <Control Id="BottomLine" Type="Line" X="0" Y="234"
Width="370" Height="0" />
      </Dialog>
    </UI>
  </Fragment>
</Wix>
```

4. Add another dialog and call it ExistingDatabase.wxs. It will be used in the event of the user choosing to use an existing database. Update its Dialog element so that it has Id of ExistingDatabaseDlg. Also, change its Title control so that it says Existing Database Screen:

```
<?xml version="1.0" encoding="UTF-8"?>
<Wix xmlns="http://schemas.microsoft.com/wix/2006/wi">
  <Fragment>
    <UI>
      <Dialog Id="ExistingDatabaseDlg" Width="370" Height="270"
Title="My Custom Dialog">
        <Control Id="Next" Type="PushButton" X="236" Y="243"
Width="56" Height="17" Default="yes" Text="!(loc.WixUINext)" />
        <Control Id="Back" Type="PushButton" X="180" Y="243"
Width="56" Height="17" Text="!(loc.WixUIBack)" />
        <Control Id="Cancel" Type="PushButton" X="304" Y="243"
Width="56" Height="17" Cancel="yes" Text="!(loc.WixUICancel)">
          <Publish Event="SpawnDialog" Value="CancelDlg">1</
Publish>
        </Control>

        <Control Id="Description" Type="Text" X="25" Y="23"
Width="280" Height="15" Transparent="yes" NoPrefix="yes"
Text="Specify an existing database" />
        <Control Id="Title" Type="Text" X="15" Y="6" Width="200"
Height="15" Transparent="yes" NoPrefix="yes" Text="Existing
Database" />
        <Control Id="BannerBitmap" Type="Bitmap" X="0"
Y="0" Width="370" Height="44" TabSkip="no" Text="!(loc.
InstallDirDlgBannerBitmap)" />
        <Control Id="BannerLine" Type="Line" X="0" Y="44"
Width="370" Height="0" />
        <Control Id="BottomLine" Type="Line" X="0" Y="234"
Width="370" Height="0" />
      </Dialog>
    </UI>
  </Fragment>
</Wix>
```

How to do it...

Add the `Publish` elements for each dialog the user could be taken to and decide which to use based on conditions within these elements. Follow the given steps to do so:

1. On the `DatabaseChoice` dialog, we want to ask the question: create a new database or use an existing one? Then beneath it add a radio button for each choice, as shown in the following markup:

```
<Control Id="Title"
         Type="Text"
         X="15"
         Y="6"
         Width="200"
         Height="15"
         Transparent="yes"
         NoPrefix="yes" Text="Database Location" />

<Control Id="Description"
         Type="Text"
         X="25"
         Y="23"
         Width="280"
         Height="15"
         Transparent="yes"
         NoPrefix="yes"
         Text="Create a new database or use an existing one?" />

<Control Id="DatabaseRadioButtons"
         Type="RadioButtonGroup"
         Property="DatabaseChosen"
         X="20"
         Y="60"
         Width="200"
         Height="100">
  <RadioButtonGroup Property="DatabaseChosen">
    <RadioButton Value="new_database"
                 Text="Create new database"
                 Width="200"
                 Height="17"
                 X="0"
                 Y="0" />
    <RadioButton Value="existing_database"
                 Text="Use existing database"
                 Width="200"
```

```
                        Height="17"
                        X="0"
                        Y="20"/>
   </RadioButtonGroup>
```

2. Add a property to the project that will select one of the radio buttons as the default. Its ID should match the `Property` attribute on the `RadioButtonGroup` `Control` element and the `Property` attribute on the `RadioButtonGroup` element. Its value selects which of the `RadioButton` elements to use as the default:

```
<Property Id="DatabaseChosen"
          Value="new" />
```

3. Go to the `CustomInstallDir.wxs` file and update it so that it has two `Publish` elements that control the `Next` button for the `DatabaseChoice` dialog. The first, which navigates to the `NewDatabaseDlg` dialog, should contain the condition `DatabaseChosen = "new"`. The second, which navigates to the `ExistingDatabaseDlg` dialog, should contain the condition `DatabaseChosen = "existing"`. Use the following markup:

```
<Publish Dialog="DatabaseChoiceDlg"
         Control="Next"
         Event="NewDialog"
         Value="NewDatabaseDlg"
         Order="1">
  DatabaseChosen = "new"
</Publish>

<Publish Dialog="DatabaseChoiceDlg"
         Control="Next"
         Event="NewDialog"
         Value="ExistingDatabaseDlg"
         Order="2">
  DatabaseChosen = "existing"
</Publish>
```

4. Be sure to update the **Back** and **Next** buttons for our `NewDatabase` and `ExistingDatabase` screens too:

```
<Publish Dialog="NewDatabaseDlg"
         Control="Back"
         Event="NewDialog"
         Value="DatabaseChoiceDlg"
         Order="1">1</Publish>

<Publish Dialog="NewDatabaseDlg"
         Control="Next"
         Event="NewDialog"
         Value="VerifyReadyDlg"
         Order="1">1</Publish>
```

```
<Publish Dialog="ExistingDatabaseDlg"
        Control="Back"
        Event="NewDialog"
        Value="DatabaseChoiceDlg"
        Order="1">1</Publish>

<Publish Dialog="ExistingDatabaseDlg"
        Control="Next"
        Event="NewDialog"
        Value="VerifyReadyDlg"
        Order="1">1</Publish>
```

5. Add the following lines to the Product.wxs file:
    ```
    <UIRef Id="CustomInstallDir"/>
    <Property Id="WIXUI_INSTALLDIR" Value="INSTALLFOLDER" />
    ```

6. Launch the installer to verify that choosing a different radio button on the
    `DatabaseChoice` dialog will change where the **Next** button takes you:

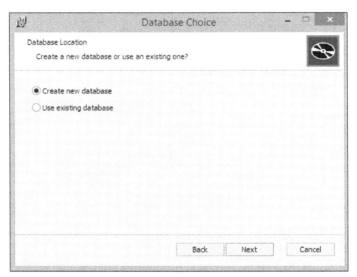

How it works...

A lot of this recipe went toward setting the stage: getting the radio buttons in place, defining a
property to hold the value of the radio buttons, and adding the new dialogs to the wizard. The
trick to show one dialog or another happened in the blink of an eye. It was when we added two
`Publish` elements to the `CustomInstallDir.wxs` file:

```
<Publish Dialog="DatabaseChoiceDlg"
        Control="Next"
        Event="NewDialog"
        Value="NewDatabaseDlg"
```

```
          Order="1">
     DatabaseChosen = "new_database"
  </Publish>

  <Publish Dialog="DatabaseChoiceDlg"
          Control="Next"
          Event="NewDialog"
          Value="ExistingDatabaseDlg"
          Order="2">
     DatabaseChosen = "existing_database"
  </Publish>
```

Ordinarily, we'd only have one `Publish` element for the **Next** button. In this case, we have two, but only one is going to get the opportunity to take the user to the dialog specified in its `Value` attribute. As you saw, the `NewDialog` event causes the current dialog to be replaced with the one specified in the `Publish` element's `Value` attribute. Which `Publish` element wins depends on what our `DatabaseChoice` property gets set to.

Each `Publish` element has a condition that checks the value of the `DatabaseChoice` property. The first checks if it has been set to `new_database` and the second checks if it has been set to `existing_database`. Also notice that each `Publish` element has an `Order` attribute. This sets up which `Publish` element will be evaluated first. If its condition evaluates to `true`, the wizard will navigate to that screen. Otherwise, the next `Publish` element gets a chance to check its condition and navigate the user to its screen.

Setting a property based on user input

There are many user interface controls at your disposal including textboxes, radio buttons, and checkboxes. The following MSDN article lists them all: `http://msdn.microsoft.com/en-us/library/aa368039(v=vs.85).aspx`. Although there are a few that are static and can't be interacted with, such as the `Text` control, which is simply a label, most of them take in and store input from the user. Those that can be interacted with use `Property` elements to store that data.

In this recipe, we'll cover one of the most useful controls: the `Edit` control, which is a textbox. We'll see how to save its value to a `Property` so that it can be used during later parts of the install. This is the same general pattern that can be applied to the other controls.

Getting ready

To prepare for this recipe, perform the following steps:

1. Create a new setup project and call it `StoringInputInstaller`.

2. As described in earlier recipes, reference `UIExtension` and add one of the default wizards. Then, add a custom dialog to the project and override the navigation of the wizard so that your dialog is displayed. During this recipe, we will add a textbox to the dialog so that we can collect user input and store it in a property.

How to do it...

Set the `Control` element's `Property` attribute so that the value of the control will be saved to a property with that name. Here's an example:

1. Add a `Control` element to the dialog that will display a textbox in which the user can enter data . Set its `Property` attribute to the `Id` of a Property element in which to store the data:

```
<Control  Id="MyTextbox"
          Type="Edit"
          Property="MY_PROPERTY"
          X="20"
          Y="80"
          Width="100"
          Height="17" />
```

2. Run the installer with logging turned on and then check the log to see that a property called MY_PROPERTY was created and set to whatever you typed into the textbox:

```
Action 21:13:43: MyCustomDlg. Dialog created

MSI (c) (C4:74) [21:13:59:428]: PROPERTY CHANGE: Adding MY_
PROPERTY property. Its value is 'test'.
```

How it works...

This example is a representative of all the `Control` elements that accept user input. It has a `Property` attribute that collects the user's input and stores it in a property with that name. If the property doesn't exist, it will be created. You can also set a default value for the control by declaring a `Property` element with a matching ID ahead of time. The following `Property` element sets a default value for our `Edit` control:

```
<Property Id="MY_PROPERTY" Value="my default value" />
```

Note that our property's ID is all uppercase. Only uppercase properties can be passed from the UI sequence to the execute sequence.

8

Users and Groups

In this chapter, we will cover the following recipes:

- ▶ Creating a local user
- ▶ Adding a new user to a new group
- ▶ Adding a new user to an existing group
- ▶ Adding an existing user to a new group
- ▶ Adding a new user with the log on as a service security setting

Introduction

In Windows, the resources that a person can access, such as files and folders, are restricted by that person's user account and the groups that they're a member of. The same goes for running processes since they adopt the privileges of whichever user launched them or in the case of long-running, self-starting services, the user account they're configured to start under. On every file and folder, there's a list of exactly who can read, modify, and execute its contents.

To fit into this paradigm, WiX lets us update the accounts and group memberships of both new and existing users. This way, we can sync a user's permissions with those required by a resource. In this chapter, we'll cover several common scenarios involving users and groups.

Creating a local user

There are plenty of times when you'll want to add a new user account for your software to use. For example, a Windows service can be run as a user whose password never expires and has access to only the parts of the system needed by your software. The same goes for a website in IIS. You must decide which user these long-running processes will run as, but they'll typically it will be a service account that only the machine interacts with. Our installer can set up a new local user on the target machine for exactly this purpose.

 When I say local user, I am referring to an account that is local to the target computer and not a domain user or a Microsoft Live account.

Getting ready

To prepare for this recipe, create a new setup project and name it `NewUserInstaller`.

How to do it...

A `User` element from the `UtilExtension` namespace can be used to create a local user account, as shown in the following steps:

1. Add `UtilExtension` to the project by right-clicking on the **References** node in **Solution Explorer** and going to **Add Reference... | WixUtilExtension.dll | Add | OK**.

2. Add the `UtilExtension` namespace to the `Wix` element:

   ```
   <Wix xmlns="http://schemas.microsoft.com/wix/2006/wi"
   xmlns:util="http://schemas.microsoft.com/wix/UtilExtension">
   ```

3. Add a `util:User` element within a `Component` element. Set its `Name` attribute to the name of the new user you'd like to create and be sure to set the component's `KeyPath` attribute to `yes`:

   ```
   <Component Id="cmpAddUser"
              Guid="{2BF75950-F6C9-44F7-90FC-B4CCBC7CC22F}"
              KeyPath="yes">
     <util:User Id="myNewUser"
             Name="Joe"
             Password="myPassword123"
             PasswordNeverExpires="yes"
             UpdateIfExists="yes" />
   </Component>
   ```

How it works...

The `UtilExtension` namespace has an element called `User` that we can leverage to add a new user account to a computer. Although the only required attributes are `Id` and `Name`, we also assigned a password that will never expire and instructed the installer to update the account if it already exists. After running the MSI, we'll be able to see the newly created account on a Windows 8 machine by opening the Windows file explorer, right-clicking on **This PC**, and going to **Manage | Local Users and Groups | Users**:

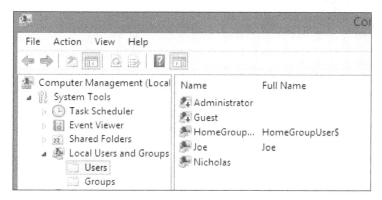

When our software is uninstalled, this user account will also be removed. However, if you want to keep it permanently, set the `User` element's `RemoveOnUninstall` attribute to `no`.

Adding a new user to a new group

A Windows group is a collection of users who have the same permissions, via the group, to a resource. This makes updating permissions easier and also lets us move users from one group to another to change their access. For example, you could add a user to a `Supervisors` group to give them full access to your software, including administration utilities; alternatively, you could add them to an `Employees` group to restrict their access to only certain files and folders. In this recipe, we'll begin by creating a user and a group and then add that user to the group.

The `UtilExtension` namespace that ships with the WiX Toolset offers a lot of functionality around users and groups, but one thing it doesn't have is a way to create a Windows group. For that, we turn to Community MSI Extensions from AppSecInc. There are several extensions in this library, but the one we're after is called `UserPrivilegesExtension`. It has elements to create users and groups.

Getting ready

To prepare for this recipe, create a new setup project called `NewUserAndGroupInstaller`.

How to do it...

Use the `UserPrivilegesExtension` from Community MSI Extensions to add a new user to a new group. The following steps show how this can be done:

1. Download Community MSI Extensions from `http://dblock.github.io/msiext/`:

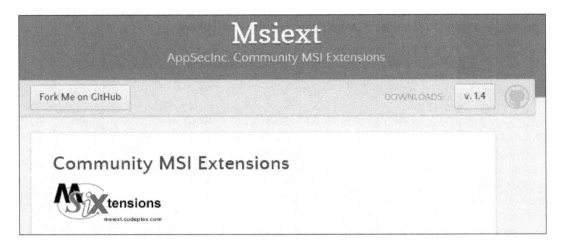

2. Unzip the downloaded ZIP file and open its `WixExtensions` folder. Copy `WixUserPrivilegesExtension.dll` to your setup project's folder.

3. Using **Solution Explorer**, add the `WixUserPrivilegesExtension.dll` file as a project reference.

4. Add the `UserPrivilegesExtension` XML namespace to the `Wix` element:

```
<Wix xmlns="http://schemas.microsoft.com/wix/2006/wi"
xmlns:userPrivs="http://schemas.appsecinc.com/wix/
UserPrivilegesExtension">
```

5. Create a new user with the `LocalUser` element from Community MSI Extensions, placing it within a component that has its `KeyPath` attribute set to `yes`:

```
<Component Id="cmpNewUserAndGroup"
           Guid="{1D8900F0-94C4-444C-8CF5-2B3C661E373C}"
           KeyPath="yes">
  <userPrivs:LocalUser Id="myLocalUser"
                       Username="Joe"
                       CreateOnInstall="yes"
                       DeleteOnUnInstall="yes"
                       CheckIfExists="yes" />
</Component>
```

6. To create a new group, add a `LocalGroup` element inside a separate component. Make sure to set the `Component` element's `KeyPath` attribute:

```
<Component Id="cmpNewGroup"
           Guid="{18D99888-67FA-4F96-8FEC-D633D0F87302}"
           KeyPath="yes">
  <userPrivs:LocalGroup Id="supervisorsGroup"
                        Name="Supervisors"
                        Description="Supervises things"
                        CreateOnInstall="yes"
                        DeleteOnUnInstall="yes"
                        CheckIfExists="yes" />
</Component>
```

7. Add the user to the group by placing a `LocalGroupMember` element that references the `LocalUser` element inside `LocalGroup`. Note that we cannot associate a user that was created with the `User` element from `UtilExtension` with the `LocalGroupMember` element:

```
<userPrivs:LocalGroup ...>
  <userPrivs:LocalGroupMember Id="AddJoeToGroup"
                              UserId="myLocalUser"
                              AddOnInstall="yes"
                              RemoveOnUnInstall="yes" />
</userPrivs:LocalGroup>
```

How it works...

Although we've already seen a way to create a user with the `User` element from `UtilExtension`, that way won't mix well with the other elements from Community MSI Extensions. If we plan to create a group and associate a user with it, we must use the `LocalUser` element instead. Its `CheckIfExists` attribute ensures the user will only be created if it doesn't already exist.

 You can find more information about the `LocalUser`, `LocalGroup`, and `LocalGroupMember` elements at `http://dblock.github.io/msiext/docs/1.4`.

The `LocalGroup` element creates a new group on the computer. Use its `Name` attribute to set the name of the group and `Description` to explain what the group is for. Then to add our user `Joe` to the group, place a `LocalGroupMember` element inside `LocalGroup`. Its `UserId` attribute should match the ID of the `LocalUser` element.

On Windows 8, you can see a list of users that are installed by opening the Windows file explorer, right-clicking on **This PC**, and going to **Manage** | **Local Users and Groups** | **Users**. After running the MSI, you should see that our user Joe has been added to the group **Supervisors**:

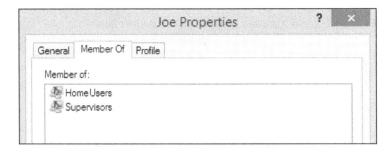

Adding a new user to an existing group

After creating a new user, you may want to add them to a group that already exists on the computer. For example, members of the Users group can do basic things such as run applications and access local and network printers. Adding your user to this group is a quick way to give them this limited access. It's pretty simple to do this using the UtilExtension namespace, as we'll see.

Getting ready

To prepare for this recipe, add a new setup project and name it NewUserExistingGroupInstaller.

How to do it...

After referencing an existing group with the Group element, add a user to it with the GroupRef element, as shown in the following steps:

1. Add UtilExtension to the project by right-clicking on the **References** node in **Solution Explorer** and going to **Add Reference...** | **WixUtilExtension.dll** | **Add** | **OK**.

2. Add the UtilExtension namespace to the Wix element:

   ```
   <Wix xmlns="http://schemas.microsoft.com/wix/2006/wi"
   xmlns:util="http://schemas.microsoft.com/wix/UtilExtension">
   ```

3. Add a Group element to reference the existing Windows group. It can be placed inside a Fragment element or within the Product element. It should not be placed in a component:

   ```
   <util:Group Id="UsersGroup" Name="Users" />
   ```

4. Add a `User` element within a component that has its `KeyPath` attribute set to yes. Set the `User` element's `Name` attribute to the name of the new user you'd like to create:

```
<Component Id="cmpAddUser"
           Guid="{2BF75950-F6C9-44F7-90FC-B4CCBC7CC22F}"
           KeyPath="yes">
  <util:User Id="myNewUser" Name="Joe" />
</Component>
```

5. Add a `GroupRef` element inside the `User` element that points to the `Group` element:

```
<util:User Id="myNewUser" Name="Joe">
  <util:GroupRef Id="UsersGroup"/>
</util:User>
```

How it works...

The `Group` element from UtilExtension doesn't create new groups, but references the existing groups found on the target computer. So, if you want to add a new user to the `Users` group, as we did in this example, you will first need to add a `Group` element with its `Name` set to `Users`.

`Users` exists on every Windows computer. However, be aware it they might not be called `Users` on non-English machines. You can solve this problem by adding a WiX localization file that contains the translation of the group name, such as for the French version. Then, you can swap your hardcoded `Name` attribute on the `Group` element for a reference to the localization variable. More information about creating a localization file can be found at `http://wixtoolset.org/documentation/manual/v3/howtos/ui_and_localization/make_installer_localizable.html`.

After referencing the group, the next step was to add our user to it by adding a `GroupRef` element inside the `User` element. The `GroupRef` element's `Id` attribute should match our `Group` element's `Id` atribute. You can stack several `GroupRef` elements to add the user to more than one group.

Adding an existing user to a new group

If you'd like to give an existing user access to your software, you'll need a way to reference their account and then add it to the group you're creating. For example, user Alice already exists on the system and you'd like to add her to a new group called `Supervisors`. As a side note, you would typically ask for that username through a UI wizard. Then, save the username to a WiX property. Properties can be accessed in other elements by using a square bracket notation, as follows:

```
<util:User Id="myNewUser" Name="[USERNAME]" />
```

The UtilExtension namespace doesn't include an element to create a new group. So, we'll return to Community MSI Extensions. In this recipe, we'll locate an existing user account and add it to our Supervisors group.

Getting ready

To prepare for this recipe, create a new setup project and call it AddExistingUserToGroupInstaller.

How to do it...

Use the elements from UserPrivilegesExtension to find an existing user and add it to a new group that you've created. The following steps show you how this is done:

1. Download Community MSI Extensions from http://dblock.github.io/msiext/.

2. Unzip the downloaded ZIP file and open its WixExtensions folder. Copy WixUserPrivilegesExtension.dll to your setup project's folder.

3. Using **Solution Explorer**, add the WixUserPrivilegesExtension.dll file as a project reference.

4. Add the UserPrivilegesExtension XML namespace to the Wix element:

```
<Wix xmlns="http://schemas.microsoft.com/wix/2006/wi"
xmlns:userPrivs="http://schemas.appsecinc.com/wix/
UserPrivilegesExtension">
```

5. Let's define a Property called USERNAME so that it's a more realistic example, wherein the username will be collected and stored in a property. This can go inside our Product element or within a fragment:

```
<Property Id="USERNAME" Value="Alice" />
```

6. Find the existing user account with the LocalUser element of UserPrivilegesExtension, setting its Username attribute to the name of the user you want to find. Since this is an existing user, set CreateOnInstall and DeleteOnUnInstall to no. Place this element within a component that has its KeyPath attribute set to yes:

```
<Component Id="cmpFindExistingUser"
           Guid="{1D8900F0-94C4-444C-8CF5-2B3C661E373C}"
           KeyPath="yes">
  <userPrivs:LocalUser Id="findLocalUser"
                       Username="[USERNAME]"
                       CreateOnInstall="no"
                       DeleteOnUnInstall="no" />
</Component>
```

7. To create a new group, add a `LocalGroup` element inside a separate component. Make sure to set the `Component` element's `KeyPath` attribute:

```
<Component Id="cmpNewGroup"
           Guid="{7BCB9259-75BB-44E8-8C08-CE4D35077047}"
           KeyPath="yes">
  <userPrivs:LocalGroup Id="supervisorsGroup"
                        Name="Supervisors"
                        Description="Supervises things"
                        CreateOnInstall="yes"
                        DeleteOnUnInstall="yes"
                        CheckIfExists="yes" />
</Component>
```

8. Add the user to the group by placing a `LocalGroupMember` element inside the `LocalGroup` element:

```
<userPrivs:LocalGroup ...>
  <userPrivs:LocalGroupMember Id="AddUserToGroup"
                              UserId="findLocalUser"
                              AddOnInstall="yes"
                              RemoveOnUnInstall="yes" />
</userPrivs:LocalGroup>
```

9. Create a user named `Alice` on the target computer and then run the installer. Verify that `Alice` was added to the `Supervisors` group.

How it works...

The `LocalUser` element will find an existing user to update, as long as we set its `CreateOnInstall` and `DeleteOnUnInstall` attributes to no. Its `Username` attribute should match the user account you're trying to find, although that name can be stored in a separate `Property` element. If you're updating the currently logged-in user, the changes won't take effect until they've logged out and back in again. To reference the current user, use the predefined `LogonUser` property, as follows:

```
<userPrivs:LocalUser Id="findCurrentUser"
                     Username="[LogonUser]"
                     CreateOnInstall="no"
                     DeleteOnUnInstall="no" />
```

As we've seen, to create a new group, we use the `LocalGroup` element. Its `Name` attribute specifies what to call the new group and `Description` sets a short explanation about it. The `CheckIfExists` attribute tells the installer to only create the group if it doesn't already exist.

To add the user to the group, we place a `LocalGroupMember` element inside `LocalGroup` and identify the user with its `UserId` attribute. By setting `AddOnInstall` and `RemoveOnUnInstall` to `yes`, we're saying that we would like the user to be added to the group during installation and removed from it during uninstallation.

Adding a new user with the log on as a service security setting

When you develop a Windows service and you want it to start automatically when the computer is turned on, you'll need to run that service as a user that has the **Log on as a service** security setting. In this recipe, you will learn how to apply this attribute to a new user account that we will create.

Getting ready

To prepare for this recipe, create a new setup project and call it `LogonAsServiceInstaller`.

How to do it...

Add the `LogonAsService` attribute to the `User` element, as outlined in the following steps:

1. Add `UtilExtension` to the project by right-clicking on the **References** node in **Solution Explorer** and going to **Add Reference...** | **WixUtilExtension.dll** | **Add** | **OK**.

2. Add the `UtilExtension` namespace to the `Wix` element:

    ```
    <Wix xmlns="http://schemas.microsoft.com/wix/2006/wi"
    xmlns:util="http://schemas.microsoft.com/wix/UtilExtension">
    ```

3. Add a `User` element within a component and set its `Name` attribute to the name of the new user you'd like to create. Set its `LogonAsService` attribute to `yes`. Be sure to set the `Component` element's `KeyPath` attribute to `yes`:

    ```
    <Component Id="cmpNewUser"
               Guid="{2CFE6625-C866-483F-B3D6-614555743069}"
               KeyPath="yes">
      <util:User Id="myNewUser"
            Name="Joe"
            UpdateIfExists="yes"
            LogonAsService="yes" />
    </Component>
    ```

How it works...

After giving a new user the ability to log on as a service, it will be able to start up and run in the background while you're logged on with your own user account. Setting it up is as simple as adding the `LogonAsService` attribute to the `User` element.

You can verify that this setting has been added by opening the **Security Settings Extension** snap-in and checking that our user, `Joe`, has been added to the **Log on as a service** assignment. In Windows 8, open **Control Panel** and then navigate to **Administrative Tools** | **Local Security Policy** | **Local Policies** | **User Rights Assignment** | **Log on as a service**. You should see `Joe` among the entries:

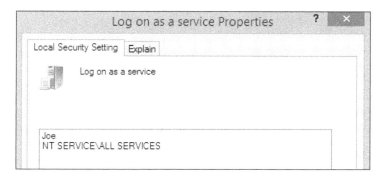

9

Handling Prerequisites

In this chapter, we will cover the following recipes:

- ▶ Stopping the installation with a launch condition
- ▶ Installing only to supported versions of Windows
- ▶ Redistributing the .NET Framework with a bootstrapper
- ▶ Executing either a 64-bit or 32-bit MSI depending on the user's operating system
- ▶ Downloading resources from the Web with a web installer

Introduction

We have several options when it comes to handling prerequisites needed by our installer. When I say prerequisites, I mean frameworks such as .NET, databases such as SQL Server, and the environment itself such as having the expected version of Windows. We can stop the installation outright if our requirements aren't met. On the other hand, in some cases, we may choose to download the missing items. For example, if the end user is missing the .NET Framework, we can install it prior to installing our own software.

In this chapter, we'll cover several scenarios, including how to prevent installations to the wrong environment, download components from the Web, and install either 32-bit or 64-bit files depending on which architecture the operating system supports.

Stopping the installation with a launch condition

A launch condition checks the user's computer to make sure that it can support our software. If it can't, the installation is automatically stopped before the user can go any further. For example, we may want to prevent the installation if the user doesn't have the necessary version of .NET installed. In this recipe, we'll do just that by adding a condition that checks for .NET Framework 4.5.

Windows 8 comes with .NET 4.5 preinstalled, but Windows 7 doesn't. We can use `NetFxExtension` to check whether .NET 4.5 is preinstalled, and if it's missing, a message is displayed telling the user that the installation cannot continue. A nice thing about launch conditions is the ability to show the user a warning message explaining what went wrong.

Getting ready

To get started, perform the following steps:

1. Create a new setup project and name it `LaunchConditionInstaller`.

2. Add a reference to `NetFxExtension` by right-clicking on the **References** node in **Solution Explorer** and going to **Add Reference... | WixNetFxExtension.dll | Add | OK**.

3. Add a `PropertyRef` element that has an ID of `NETFRAMEWORK45`. This can go inside the `Product` element and gives us access to that property, which is defined in the `WixNetFxExtension.dll` library:

   ```
   <PropertyRef Id="NETFRAMEWORK45"/>
   ```

How to do it...

Use a `Condition` element to prevent the installation from continuing if its conditional statement evaluates to `false`. The following steps show how to do it:

1. Add a `Condition` element inside the `Product` element. Its `Message` attribute defines what the user will see if the condition is `false`:

   ```
   <Condition Message="You must install Microsoft .NET Framework 4.5
   or higher">
   </Condition>
   ```

2. Inside the `Condition` element, add the conditional statement. To prevent any characters in the statement from being parsed as XML, surround it with `CDATA` tags. The following example uses the `NETFRAMEWORK45` property that's defined in `NetFxExtension` to check whether .NET 4.5 is installed. It also uses the `Installed` property to ensure the condition is only checked during a first-time installation:

```
<Condition Message="You must install Microsoft .NET Framework 4.5
or higher">
    <![CDATA[Installed OR NETFRAMEWORK45]]>
</Condition>
```

3. Compile and run the installer on a computer that does not have the .NET Framework 4.5 to see the warning message, as shown in the following screenshot:

How it works...

The `Condition` element creates a `launch` condition in our installer. If the statement nested inside evaluates to `false`, then our warning message will be displayed to the user and the installation will stop. This check happens very early in the installation process, even before a UI wizard has been shown. So, it can't be used to validate a user's input. However, it can check for the version of the operating system, whether a particular version of software is installed, or any other check that relies on information already present in the system.

In this example, we looked for a property called `NETFRAMEWORK45`, which is only set if the .NET Framework 4.5 is present. If you were to keep a log of the installation, you'd see that the `NETFRAMEWORK45` property is set to a release number if it's found, shown as follows:

MSI (c) (F4:60) [17:27:51:193]: PROPERTY CHANGE: Adding NETFRAMEWORK45 property. Its value is '#378758'.

If .NET 4.5 is not found, the condition is `false` and the warning message is displayed. You can learn more about properties for other versions of .NET, as defined by `NetFxExtension`, at `http://wixtoolset.org/documentation/manual/v3/customactions/wixnetfxextension.html#properties`.

When developing your own properties for use in the `launch` conditions, you'll often make use of the AppSearch queries. AppSearch is an umbrella term that includes searching the registry and filesystem to get clues about whether some third-party tool is installed. For example, you might check to see if Notepad++ is installed by searching for `notepad++.exe` in `Program Files`. That's the sort of thing that `NetFxExtension` does. You can get a better idea about how it works by reading about the `RegistrySearch` element at `http://wixtoolset.org/documentation/manual/v3/howtos/files_and_registry/read_a_registry_entry.html`.

We also included `Installed OR` in our condition, so that our check for the .NET Framework will only be done if this is a first-time installation. This way, there's no chance that we'll inadvertently prevent the user from uninstalling our software.

There's more...

In this recipe, we added a single launch condition to check whether the .NET Framework 4.5 is installed. If you wanted to add more conditions, simply add more `Condition` elements. Note that you can't ever know the order in which these conditions will be evaluated, so try to think of each of them as being equally important. The following example checks for .NET 4.5 and SQL Server 2014 Express:

```
<Condition Message="You must install Microsoft .NET Framework 4.5 or
higher">
  <![CDATA[Installed OR NETFRAMEWORK45]]>
</Condition>
<Condition Message="You must have SQL Server 2014 Express installed">
  <![CDATA[Installed OR SQL_EXPRESS2014]]>
</Condition>
```

To find out whether SQL Server Express is installed, we look for a property called `SQL_EXPRESS2014`. We can use the `RegistrySearch` element to read the Windows registry and set this property. Here's how it is done:

```
<Property Id="SQL_EXPRESS2014">
  <RegistrySearch Id="SearchForSqlExpress"
                  Root="HKLM"
                  Key="SOFTWARE\Microsoft\Microsoft SQL Server\
SQLEXPRESS\MSSQLServer\CurrentVersion"
                  Name="CurrentVersion"
                  Type="raw" />
</Property>
```

Note that whether our search finds the 32-bit or 64-bit SQL Server Express depends on which architecture our installer targets. If we build our installer to target a 32-bit architecture, it will not see keys in the 64-bit section of the registry. This is handled automatically by the `RegistrySearch` element.

Installing only to supported versions of Windows

Once we're confident that our application works on a particular version of Windows, we may want to prevent users from installing to other unsupported operating systems. Here, we can use a `launch` condition. Launch conditions evaluate the state of the user's system and then cancel the installation if our requirements aren't met. By checking the operating system version, we can save the end user from trying to use our software on a system it was never intended for.

Getting ready

Create a new setup project and name it `SupportedWindowsInstaller`.

How to do it...

Add a `launch` condition that checks the `VersionNT` property to see what the computer's version of Windows is:

1. Add a `Condition` element inside the `Product` element. Its `Message` attribute will explain that the current operating system is not supported, as follows:

   ```
   <Condition Message="Only Windows 8 and up is supported">
   </Condition>
   ```

2. Add a conditional statement inside that element that compares the `VersionNT` property to a Windows version number in the form of *major version * 100 + minor version*. So, version 6.2 would be 602, as shown in the following code:

   ```
   <Condition Message="Only Windows 8 and up is supported">
     <![CDATA[Installed OR VersionNT >= 602]]>
   </Condition>
   ```

3. If you attempt to install this to Windows 7, you'll see the following warning:

How it works...

The `Condition` element creates what's called a launch condition in our installer. It prevents the user from installing our software if the given conditional statement evaluates to `false`. In this case, we're using the built-in `VersionNT` property to check for a specific version of Windows. The following table, which you can also find online at `http://msdn.microsoft.com/en-us/library/aa370556(v=vs.85).aspx`, lists the possible values of `VersionNT`:

Operating System	VersionNT
Windows 2000	500
Windows XP	501
Windows Server 2003	502
Windows Vista	600
Windows 7 / Windows Server 2008	601
Windows 8 / Windows Server 2012	602
Windows 8.1	603

Our condition compares `VersionNT` to 602 using a greater-than or equal-to sign:

```
VersionNT >= 602
```

This means that we'll support Windows 8 or newer operating systems. You can find information about other comparison operators at `http://msdn.microsoft.com/en-us/library/aa368012%28v=vs.85%29.aspx`.

Using these operators, we can check for a variety of scenarios. For example, we can see whether the current operating system is Windows XP through Windows 7 by placing AND between two statements, as follows:

```
VersionNT >= 501 AND VersionNT <= 601
```

There's more...

The `VersionNT` property gives us the version of Windows that's installed, but if we want to get really fine-grained, we can combine it with the `ServicePackLevel` property. It tells us which service packs have been installed. For example, if we wanted to know whether the current operating system is Windows 7 with Service Pack 1, we could write the following condition:

```
<Condition Message="Only Windows 7 Service Pack 1 is supported">
  <![CDATA[VersionNT = 601 AND ServicePackLevel = 1]]>
</Condition>
```

You can also determine whether the system is a 64-bit one by checking for the `VersionNT64` property. It's only set on a 64-bit machine.

Redistributing the .NET Framework with a bootstrapper

A bootstrapper checks for prerequisites and installs them if they're missing. So, we could install .NET or SQL Server if it's not present and then follow up by installing our own software. WiX Toolset adds a Visual Studio project template called **Bootstrapper Project**. In this recipe, we'll see how to deploy the .NET Framework with it.

Getting ready

Create a new setup project and call it `InstallerThatNeedsDotNet`. We'll use a bootstrapper to bundle this MSI with the .NET Framework.

How to do it...

Add a bootstrapper project, reference `NetFxExtension` within it, and then include one of its .NET packages in the bootstrapper:

1. Add a **Bootstrapper Project** to the solution by right-clicking on the solution in **Solution Explorer** and going to **Add** | **New Project...** | **Windows Installer XML** | **Bootstrapper Project** | **OK**:

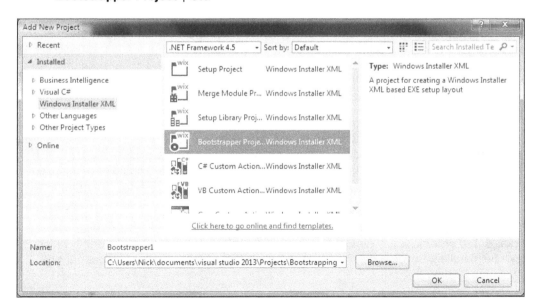

2. `NetFxExtension` contains packages to install .NET. Add it to the project by right-clicking on the **References** node in **Solution Explorer** and going to **Add Reference...** | **WixNetFxExtension.dll** | **Add** | **OK**.

3. To include a specific .NET package, update the `Bundle.wxs` file by adding a `PackageGroupRef` element inside its `Chain` element. Set the `PackageGroupRef` element's `Id` attribute to one of the .NET package groups defined in `NetFxExtension`, such as `NetFx45Redist`, which installs .NET 4.5:

```
<Chain>
  <PackageGroupRef Id="NetFx45Redist"/>
</Chain>
```

4. Have the bootstrapper also install our MSI by including it within the `Chain` element after `PackageGroupRef`. The order of elements in `Chain` is the order in which they'll be installed. If you add your setup project as a reference in the bootstrapper project, you can use the `$(var.NameofProject.TargetDir)` preprocessor variable as follows:

```
<Chain>
  <PackageGroupRef Id="NetFx45Redist"/>
  <MsiPackage SourceFile="$(var.InstallerThatNeedsDotNet.
TargetDir)InstallerThatNeedsDotNet.msi" />
</Chain>
```

How it works...

A **Bootstrapper Project** allows us to chain together installation packages and execute them sequentially. When it comes to installing the .NET Framework, we can download the .NET redistributable, define the proper elements to add it to our bootstrapper, and then set all the necessary flags to run the package silently without triggering a computer restart. However, the easier option is to do what we've done here, that is, reference `NetFxExtension` and use one of its .NET packages groups. This way, all the heavy lifting is done for us. All we have to do is add a `PackageGroupRef` element.

A `PackageGroupRef` references a `PackageGroup` element. `PackageGroup` may contain other bootstrapper elements and is similar to `Fragment` in a setup project. It lets us split our bootstrapper elements into modular chunks. Those from `NetFxExtension` contain .NET redistributables. We used the one used for installing .NET 4.5, but we could have installed .NET 4 by referencing the `NetFx40Redist` `PackageGroup`, or .NET 4.5.1 by referencing `NetFx451Redist`.

After adding the .NET Framework to our bootstrapper, we followed it in `Chain` with our MSI package. The order in which elements appear in the `Chain` element is the order in which they'll be installed. So, our bootstrapper ensures .NET 4.5 will be present before our MSI installation begins.

When you run the bootstrapper, you'll see that it informs us that it's installing the .NET Framework, as shown in the following screenshot:

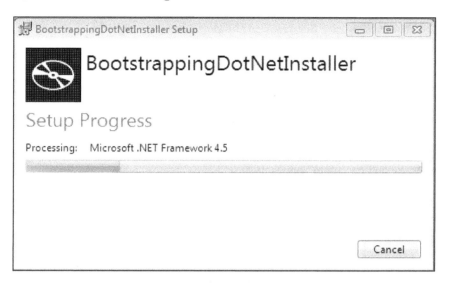

Executing either a 64-bit or 32-bit MSI depending on the user's operating system

An MSI can target a 64-bit or 32-bit processor architecture, but never both. An MSI contains metadata called **Template Summary** that denotes which architecture it supports, and it can only support one or the other at a time. However, there is a way to give the user a single package that will install either 64-bit or 32-bit software, depending on their operating system. In this recipe, we will build such a package, combining both architectures into a single bootstrapper bundle.

Getting ready

To prepare for this recipe, follow these steps:

1. Create two new setup projects within the same Visual Studio solution. The first is our 32-bit installer and is called `ThirtyTwoBitInstaller`. It targets `ProgramFilesFolder` in its directory structure:

    ```
    <Directory Id="TARGETDIR" Name="SourceDir">
      <Directory Id="ProgramFilesFolder">
        <Directory Id="INSTALLFOLDER"
                   Name="ThirtyTwoBitInstaller" />
      </Directory>
    </Directory>
    ```

2. The second, which is our 64-bit installer, is called `SixtyFourBitInstaller` and targets `ProgramFiles64Folder`:

```
<Directory Id="TARGETDIR" Name="SourceDir">
  <Directory Id="ProgramFiles64Folder">
    <Directory Id="INSTALLFOLDER"
               Name="SixtyFourBitInstaller" />
  </Directory>
</Directory>
```

3. For the 64-bit installer, add `-arch x64` to the project's `Compiler` parameters found by right-clicking on the project and going to **Properties | Tool Settings**.

4. Add at least one file to each project, such as a text file. Without something to install, an MSI won't complete successfully.

How to do it...

Include both MSIs in a bootstrapper. Use the `InstallCondition` attribute on the `MsiPackage` element to install only one of them:

1. Add **Bootstrapper Project** to the solution by right-clicking on the solution in **Solution Explorer** and going to **Add | New Project... | Windows Installer XML | Bootstrapper Project | OK**.

2. To ensure the projects are built in the correct order and also so that we can use preprocessor variables to access the compiled MSIs, add references to each of the setup projects within the bootstrapper project.

3. In the bootstrapper's `Bundle.wxs` file, add an `MsiPackage` element inside the `Chain` for `SixtyFourBitInstaller.msi`. Set its `InstallCondition` attribute to `VersionNT64`, which is only set on 64-bit machines:

```
<Chain>
  <MsiPackage InstallCondition="VersionNT64" SourceFile="$(var.
SixtyFourBitInstaller.TargetDir)SixtyFourBitInstaller.msi" />
</Chain>
```

4. Add a second `MsiPackage` element to the chain that points to `ThirtyTwoBitInstaller.msi`. Set its `InstallCondition` attribute to `NOT VersionNT64`:

```
<Chain>
  <MsiPackage ... />
  <MsiPackage InstallCondition="NOT VersionNT64"
SourceFile="$(var.ThirtyTwoBitInstaller.TargetDir)
ThirtyTwoBitInstaller.msi" />
</Chain>
```

How it works...

We began by creating two setup projects: one for a 64-bit installation and the other for a 32-bit installation. We included both in a bootstrapper by referencing each project and then adding the `MsiPackage` elements inside the `Chain` element. We gave each `MsiPackage` an `InstallCondition` that examines the `VersionNT64` variable.

`VersionNT64` will only be defined on a 64-bit operating system. Therefore, the 64-bit `MsiPackage` checks whether it has been set and the 32-bit `MsiPackage` checks whether it has *not* been set. This way, which `MsiPackage` will be deployed is a decision that's made at installation time based on the user's operating system.

When the bootstrapper runs, it will keep a log that you can find in the `%TEMP%` directory. Here, you'll be able to see that `InstallCondition` is checked for each package, as shown in the following snippet:

```
[09E0:09E4][2014-10-07T20:44:19]i052: Condition 'VersionNT64' evaluates
to true.

[09E0:09E4][2014-10-07T20:44:19]i052: Condition 'NOT VersionNT64'
evaluates to false.

[09E0:09E4][2014-10-07T20:44:19]i201: Planned package:
SixtyFourBitInstaller.msi, state: Absent, default requested: Present, ba
requested: Present, execute: Install, rollback: Uninstall, cache: Yes,
uncache: No, dependency: Register

[09E0:09E4][2014-10-07T20:44:19]i201: Planned package:
ThirtyTwoBitInstaller.msi, state: Absent, default requested: Absent, ba
requested: Absent, execute: None, rollback: None, cache: No, uncache: No,
dependency: None
```

You can see that, in this case, `VersionNT64` evaluates to `true`, whereas the condition `NOT VersionNT64` evaluates to `false`. This causes `SixtyFourBitInstaller.msi` to get the go-ahead to be installed, whereas `ThirtyTwoBitInstaller.msi` does not.

Downloading resources from the Web with a web installer

A web installer is a bootstrapper that downloads some or all of its resources from the web during installation. This way, the initial download of the bootstrapper is faster, since its file size is much smaller. The main portion of it is hosted online where it's only downloaded when you need it. The disadvantage is that end users will need an Internet connection when they run the installer. However, in many cases, that's a small price to pay.

In this recipe, we'll need to have our resources hosted online. When I say resources, I'm talking about MSI packages, other executable installers, and patch files. To give you an idea about how it would work, we'll use an MSI file that's already on the Web: the Node.js installer.

Getting ready

To prepare for this recipe, perform the following steps:

1. Create a new bootstrapper project and call it `WebInstaller`.

2. Download the Node.js MSI from `http://nodejs.org/download` and copy it to the directory of the bootstrapper project.

How to do it...

Use the `MsiPackage` element's `DownloadUrl` attribute to indicate that you'd like to download an MSI from the Web. The following steps will help you do it:

1. In the `Bundle.wxs` file, add an `MsiPackage` element to the `Chain` element. Set its `SourceFile` attribute so that it points to the Node.js MSI file you copied to the project's directory. It should also have a `DownloadUrl` attribute set to the URL, where the MSI package can be directly downloaded from the Web. At the time of writing this book, the URL was `http://nodejs.org/dist/v0.10.32/node-v0.10.32-x86.msi`. The following code snippet shows how to do so:

```
<Chain>
  <MsiPackage
    Id="NODEJS"
    SourceFile="node-v0.10.32-x86.msi"
    DownloadUrl="http://nodejs.org/dist/v0.10.32/node-v0.10.32-x86.msi" />
</Chain>
```

2. Set `Compressed` to `no` to inform the bootstrapper that it should not embed the MSI, since it's going to download it during installation. In this case, since the MSI adds files to `Program Files (x86)`, also set `ForcePerMachine` to `yes` so that the user will be prompted to elevate:

```
<Chain>
  <MsiPackage
    Id="NODEJS"
    SourceFile="node-v0.10.32-x86.msi"
    DownloadUrl="http://nodejs.org/dist/v0.10.32/node-v0.10.32-x86.msi"
    Compressed="no"
    ForcePerMachine="yes" />
</Chain>
```

3. Compile the project and look in the output folder. The MSI should not be embedded within the bootstrapper:

4. When you run `WebInstaller.exe`, you'll see that its progress bar shows it installing Node.js:

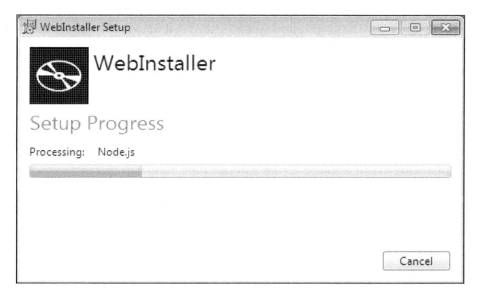

How it works...

For demonstration purposes, we needed an MSI file that's available for download on the Web. So, we used the Node.js installer. When creating a web installer for your own software, you'll need to host your MSI files online where your bootstrapper can access them. A copy of the MSI is kept local to the project, otherwise it won't compile. However, by setting `Compressed` to `no`, the compiled bootstrapper will not contain the MSI. It may retain some metadata about it, but that's all. Note that you cannot compile against one version of an MSI and then host a different version online. WiX compares a hash of the MSI packages and the bootstrapper will fail if there's a mismatch.

The `DownloadUrl` attribute defines where we can get the MSI during installation. This URL must be a direct link to the file. We also added the `ForcePerMachine` attribute, since without it the installation fails due to insufficient privileges when the Node.js installer tries to write to the `Program Files` folder. Setting `ForcePerMachine` causes Node.js to be installed for all users on the computer and gives us the permissions we need to complete the installation.

After completing the installation, if you open the installer's logfile found in the `%TEMP%` directory, you'll see that the MSI was downloaded from the Web:

```
[0584:0C70][2014-10-08T23:02:17]i338: Acquiring package: NODEJS, payload:
NODEJS, download from: http://nodejs.org/dist/v0.10.32/node-v0.10.32-x86.
msi
```

When the user uninstalls our bootstrapper, Node.js will be uninstalled with it since it's part of our bundle. However, if Node.js had already been installed, it would have been left as is. MSI packages have reference counting built in.

10
Installing Websites

In this chapter, we will cover the following recipes:

- ▶ Spinning up a new application pool in IIS
- ▶ Adding a website to IIS that runs under your app pool
- ▶ Creating a virtual directory
- ▶ Adding a web application to IIS
- ▶ Setting up a website to use SSL

Introduction

Setting up a website is often where control leaves the hands of a developer and enters the hands of a system administrator or an end user. Unfortunately, that handoff doesn't always go smoothly and things may not be configured the same way as the developer expects. With WiX, we can provide an installer that will set up everything in IIS just the way we'd like it to be. It can also ensure that development, QA, and production environments are set up consistently. In this chapter, we'll see how to install application pools, websites, and virtual directories to IIS.

Spinning up a new application pool in IIS

The first step when adding a website to IIS is to configure the application pool that it will run in. This isolates the site from others on the server for better stability and security. On the stability front, each app pool runs its own worker process that, should it die or be taken offline intentionally, won't affect the others. As for security, you can customize the user account that the app pool process runs as. This way, you can give one website more or less access than another.

Getting ready

Create a new setup project and name it `AppPoolInstaller`.

How to do it...

In this recipe, we will add a new application pool to IIS. We'll configure its name, version of the .NET CLR to use, and the user account to run as. Perform the following steps:

1. Add `IIsExtension` to the project by right-clicking on the **References** node in **Solution Explorer** and going to **Add Reference...** | **WixIIsExtension.dll** | **Add** | **OK**.

2. Add the `IIsExtension` namespace to the `Wix` element:

    ```
    <Wix xmlns="http://schemas.microsoft.com/wix/2006/wi"
    xmlns:iis="http://schemas.microsoft.com/wix/IIsExtension">
    ```

3. Add a `Component` element that has its `KeyPath` attribute set to `yes`:

    ```
    <ComponentGroup Id="ProductComponents"
                    Directory="INSTALLFOLDER">
      <Component Id="cmpAppPool"
               Guid="{CBA59BDC-989C-4F77-B0F9-861AAB8E0DEB}"
               KeyPath="yes">
      </Component>
    </ComponentGroup>
    ```

4. Add a `WebAppPool` element from `IIsExtension` inside `Component`:

    ```
    <Component ...>
      <iis:WebAppPool Id="MyAppPool"
                      Name="MyWebsiteAppPool"
                      ManagedRuntimeVersion="v4.0"
                      ManagedPipelineMode="integrated"
                      Identity="applicationPoolIdentity" />
    </Component>
    ```

How it works...

We began by adding a reference to `IIsExtension` that ships with the WiX Toolset. This extension gives us a `WebAppPool` element that will create an application pool in IIS. Although we can configure minute details of the app pool, including how often it should be recycled, the maximum number of worker processes to use, and how many requests can be queued, we can also leave them at their default settings and only set those that are most important to us.

More information about the available application pool settings can be found at `http://wixtoolset.org/documentation/manual/v3/xsd/iis/webapppool.html`.

The `Id` attribute is necessary to uniquely identify the `WebAppPool` element in the MSI. `Name` sets what to call the application pool in IIS. The `ManagedRuntimeVersion` attribute configures which version of the .NET Common Language Runtime to use. You can see it by opening the IIS manager console by going to **Run...** | **inetmgr**, selecting the **Application Pools** node, right-clicking on your app pool, and selecting **Advanced Settings...**, as shown in the following screenshot:

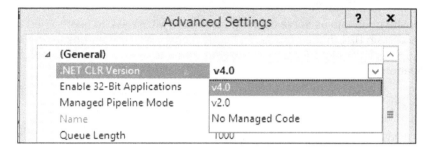

The `ManagedPipelineMode` attribute should be set to `integrated` to give modern ASP. NET websites full access to incoming requests for tasks such as authentication, caching, and other filtering handled by HTTP modules. However, if you're running a version of IIS prior to IIS 7, you can still set it to **Classic**:

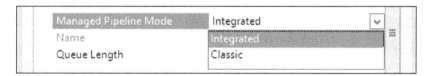

In this example, we set the `WebAppPool` element's `Identity` attribute to `applicationPoolIdentity`. This attribute sets the user account under which the app pool's worker process will run. The `applicationPoolIdentity` user, which is available in IIS 7 and later, creates a virtual account tailor-made for the application pool, limiting its access to other processes. Alternatively, you can specify one of the following built-in accounts: `localSystem`, `localService`, or `networkService`. You can also specify a custom user by setting this attribute to `other` and then adding the `User` attribute. `User` is set to the `Id` of a corresponding `User` element.

One thing to note is that if the application pool already exists, it will be updated with the new settings. However, during an uninstallation, that app pool might be removed if your installer is the only one to have installed that `Component` element. Placing `WebAppPool` within your `Product` element or directly inside `Fragment` instead of in `Component` will allow you to reference an existing application pool without creating it. However, there isn't a way to create an application pool only if it does not exist. I recommend you to always create a new, uniquely named application pool for each website.

Adding a website to IIS that runs under your app pool

Adding a website to IIS lets us serve content, such as HTML pages, to users when they navigate to a certain URL in their browsers. In this recipe, we'll add a website that contains a `Default.htm` page. IIS looks for a page with this name to display first. Our website will run in a new application pool.

Getting ready

Perform the following steps to prepare for this recipe:

1. Create a new setup project and name it `WebsiteInstaller`.

2. Add `IIsExtension` to the project by right-clicking on the **References** node in **Solution Explorer** and going to **Add Reference... | WixIIsExtension.dll | Add | OK**.

3. Add the `IIsExtension` namespace to the `Wix` element:

   ```
   <Wix xmlns="http://schemas.microsoft.com/wix/2006/wi"
   xmlns:iis="http://schemas.microsoft.com/wix/IIsExtension">
   ```

4. Add an application pool, as we did in the previous recipe, so that we can later assign our website to it. Set its `Id` attribute to `MyAppPool`.

5. Add an HTML file to the project so that we'll have a page to show when we navigate to our website. Here's a simple example that you can save as `Default.htm`:

   ```
   <!DOCTYPE html>
   <html lang="en">
     <head>
       <meta charset="utf-8" />
       <title>My Website</title>
     </head>
     <body>
       <h1>My Website</h1>
     </body>
   </html>
   ```

6. Add the `Component` and `File` elements for `Default.htm`. Be sure that it is installed in the `INSTALLFOLDER` directory by placing it within `ProductComponents` `ComponentGroup`:

```
<ComponentGroup Id="ProductComponents"
                Directory="INSTALLFOLDER">
  <Component Id="cmpDefaultHTM"
             Guid="{3032BC5D-D0DB-4007-B8C1-FFC919C4F5A5}">
    <File Source="Default.htm" />
  </Component>

  <!--Other components-->
</ComponentGroup>
```

How to do it...

The `WebSite`, `WebApplication`, and `WebAddress` elements are used to add a site to IIS, specify its application pool, and the port to use. Perform the following steps:

1. Add a `Component` element with its `KeyPath` attribute set to `yes`:

```
<Component Id="cmpMyWebsite"
           Guid="{95565B4A-C24A-4F64-9644-DE64973DE6B3}"
           KeyPath="yes">

</Component>
```

2. Within it, add a `WebSite` element from the `IIsExtension`. Set its `Description` attribute to the name of the web site as you'd like it to appear in IIS. Set its `Directory` attribute to the `Id` of a corresponding `Directory` element where the web site's files will be stored. If you think the site may already exist, set `ConfigureIfExists` to yes:

```
<iis:WebSite Id="website_MyWebsite"
             Description="MyWebsite"
             Directory="INSTALLFOLDER"
             ConfigureIfExists="yes">
</iis:WebSite>
```

3. Within the `WebSite` element, add a `WebApplication` element to set up which application pool we'll use. Its `WebAppPool` attribute should match the `Id` of our `WebAppPool` element:

```
<iis:WebSite ...>
  <iis:WebApplication Id="webapplication_MyWebsite"
                      Name="MyWebApplication"
                      WebAppPool="MyAppPool" />
</iis:WebSite>
```

4. Also within the `WebSite` element, add a `WebAddress` that specifies the port where the site will listen for incoming requests. For now, set this to port `8080`:

```
<iis:WebSite ...>
  <iis:WebApplication ... />
  <iis:WebAddress Id="webaddress_MyWebsite"
                  Port="8080" />
</iis:WebSite>
```

How it works...

After running the installer, open the IIS manager. You can do so by entering `inetmgr` in the **Run** window. Verify that our website is listed under the `Sites` folder:

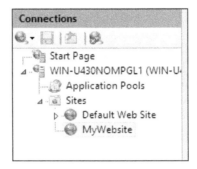

If we browse to our site at `http://localhost:8080`, we'll see our `Default.htm` page displayed:

The `Website` element from `IIsExtension` creates the new website under the `Sites` folder. Notice that its name is the same as we set for the `Website` element's `Description` attribute. We can also right-click on the **MyWebsite** node and select **Explore** to open the folder containing our HTML file, `C:\Program Files (x86)\WebsiteInstaller`, and see that our `Default.htm` file is there. The `Website` element's `Directory` attribute configured that this would be the place to find our files.

We added two other elements inside the `Website` element: `WebApplication` and `WebAddress`. The first element simply associates our website with the application pool we created earlier. Note that we specified the required `Name` attribute in the `WebApplication` element, but in this scenario, it has no bearing. The `WebAddress` element sets up the port that our site will listen to. In this example, we used port `8080` so that there's less chance of it interfering with the default website that's already installed and listening at port `80`.

There's more...

So far in this recipe, we avoided giving our website a domain name or specific IP address. As it stands, our website will be displayed if the user enters any of the following in their browser's address bar (from the same machine):

- `http://localhost:8080`

- `http://127.0.0.1:8080`

- `http://10.0.2.15:8080` (using the network IP address of the machine)

- `http://mywebsite.com:8080` (if `mywebsite.com` has been mapped with DNS to `10.0.2.15`)

The common theme is that each explicitly uses port `8080`. However, changing the port on any of these addresses to `80`, or leaving it out altogether, will bring up the default website. The reason for this is that when we configured the `WebAddress` element, we only gave it a `Port` attribute. Therefore, its port is the only thing that distinguishes it from other sites on that server:

```
<iis:WebAddress Id="webaddress_MyWebsite"
                Port="8080" />
```

If we click on the **Sites** node in the IIS manager, we can see that the `Binding` properties for the default website and our own are identical except for their ports. Both use an asterisk for the address, as shown:

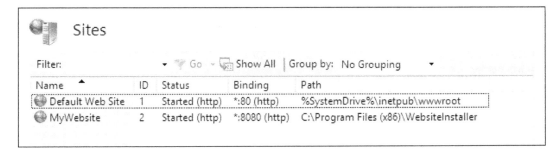

Name	ID	Status	Binding	Path
Default Web Site	1	Started (http)	*:80 (http)	%SystemDrive%\inetpub\wwwroot
MyWebsite	2	Started (http)	*:8080 (http)	C:\Program Files (x86)\WebsiteInstaller

Let's try updating the `WebAddress` element so that it specifies an IP address. I'll use `10.0.2.15`, since that's the address that's assigned to me on my network:

```
<iis:WebAddress Id="webaddress_MyWebsite"
                IP="10.0.2.15"
                Port="80" />
```

Note that we're now using port `80` instead of `8080`. After reinstalling, we'll see the following bindings:

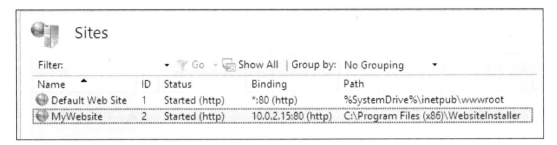

Now, any request for that IP address, such as `http://10.0.2.15:80`, or more simply, since port `80` is the default, `http://10.0.2.15` will yield `MyWebsite`:

However, a request to any other IP, such as `http://127.0.0.1`, will yield the default website. That's because the asterisk in its binding picks up any other unassigned addresses.

We can also distinguish our website by a domain name. Update the `WebAddress` element to the following:

```
<iis:WebAddress Id="webaddress_MyWebsite"
                Header="mywebsite.com"
                Port="80" />
```

Our bindings should now look like this:

Both sites use port `80` and neither claims a specific IP address. However, `MyWebsite` is bound to the `mywebsite.com` domain and will be returned for anyone who uses `mywebsite.com` in the URL, such as `http://mywebsite.com`. This is assuming that DNS has been set up to map `mywebsite.com` to this machine's IP address, which for me is `10.0.2.15`.

> You can set up DNS on a Windows server locally for testing by editing the `C:\Windows\System32\drivers\etc\hosts` file. You can also set up a DNS entry using Windows DNS Server. To learn more about setting up a DNS entry, see the following link to create a Forward Lookup Zone: `http://technet.microsoft.com/en-us/library/cc771566.aspx`; and see the following link to learn about creating a Host (A) record: `http://technet.microsoft.com/en-us/library/cc779029(v=ws.10).aspx`.
>
> You may also need to update your network adapter to use the current machine as its preferred DNS Server. More information can be found at `http://www.opennicproject.org/configure-your-dns/how-to-change-dns-servers-in-windows-7/`.

The user should see the following screen at `http://mywebsite.com`:

On the other hand, if the user enters an IP address explicitly, such as `http://10.0.2.15`, they'll get the default website. The way that requests are routed in IIS is as follows:

1. If an IP address is given, find the site that is bound to it specifically. If none is found, use the site that uses an asterisk as its IP. If more than one is bound to that IP address or if more than one uses an asterisk, move on to step 2.

2. Find the site that is bound to the given port (defaulting to port `80`). If none is found, return a response indicating that the site could not be found. If more than one is bound to that port, move on to step 3.

3. If a domain name is given, find the site that is bound to it. If none is found, return a response indicating that the site could not be found.

Creating a virtual directory

A website in IIS maps to a directory on the computer. If there are subdirectories within that folder, they'll show up in the IIS manager too. For example, the following website has the `Scripts` and `CSS` folders inside its root folder:

If we right-click on **MyWebsite** and choose **Explore**, we'll see that the `Scripts` and `CSS` directories sit squarely within the folder that the site is mapped to:

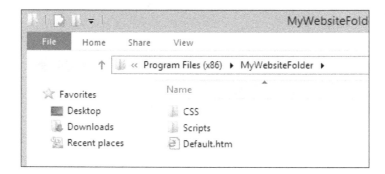

What if we wanted to map to a directory that wasn't within the root folder of the website? Maybe it's a folder at `C:\Photos`. To do this, we'll need to create a virtual directory. A virtual directory simply maps to some place outside the normal website folder. In this recipe, we will add a `Photos` directory to the `C:` drive and map it as a virtual directory in IIS.

Getting ready

To prepare for this recipe, perform the following steps:

1. Create a new setup project and name it `VirtualDirectoryInstaller`.

2. Add `IIsExtension` to the project by right-clicking on the **References** node in **Solution Explorer** and going to **Add Reference... | WixIIsExtension.dll | Add | OK**.

3. Add the `IIsExtension` namespace to the `Wix` element:

   ```
   <Wix xmlns="http://schemas.microsoft.com/wix/2006/wi"
   xmlns:iis="http://schemas.microsoft.com/wix/IIsExtension">
   ```

4. Add an application pool, as discussed previously.

5. Add a website, as discussed in the previous recipe.

6. Now, we can compare regular website directories to virtual directories; add the CSS and `Scripts` folders using the `Directory` elements:

   ```
   <Directory Id="INSTALLFOLDER"
              Name="VirtualDirectoryInstaller">
     <Directory Id="CssFolder" Name="CSS" />
     <Directory Id="ScriptsFolder" Name="Scripts" />
   </Directory>
   ```

7. Add a component for each with `CreateFolder` inside so that they'll be created even though they're empty. These should be placed outside the existing `ProductComponents ComponentGroup`, since they declare their own `Directory` attributes:

   ```
   <Component Id="cmpCssFolder"
              Guid="{6E68FAE5-A498-4331-BABE-AF456CA245E3}"
              KeyPath="yes"
              Directory="CssFolder">
     <CreateFolder />
   </Component>

   <Component Id="cmpScriptsFolder"
              Guid="{E27D57AA-9507-40C3-B1F6-0A1238AD191B}"
              KeyPath="yes"
              Directory="ScriptsFolder">
     <CreateFolder />
   </Component>
   ```

8. Reference these components inside our `Feature` element so that they'll be included in the installation:

```
<Feature Id="ProductFeature" Title="VirtualDirectoryInstaller"
Level="1">
  <ComponentGroupRef Id="ProductComponents" />
  <ComponentRef Id="cmpCssFolder"/>
  <ComponentRef Id="cmpScriptsFolder"/>
</Feature>
```

How to do it...

Register a folder as a virtual directory by using the `WebVirtualDir` element, as shown in the following steps:

1. Add the `Directory` element, which will become our virtual directory. In this case, we'll call it `PhotosDir` and place it within the `TARGETDIR` folder. This way, it will be created directly on the `C:` drive:

```
<Directory Id="TARGETDIR" Name="SourceDir">
  <Directory Id="ProgramFilesFolder">
    <Directory Id="INSTALLFOLDER"
              Name="VirtualDirectoryInstaller">
      <Directory Id="CssFolder" Name="CSS" />
      <Directory Id="ScriptsFolder" Name="Scripts" />
    </Directory>
  </Directory>

  <Directory Id="PhotosDir" Name="Photos" />
</Directory>
```

2. Add a `Component` with a `CreateFolder` element inside it to create the new directory. `CreateFolder` ensures that it will be installed even though it is empty. Alternatively, add a few files to the folder:

```
<Component Id="cmpPhotosFolder"
          Guid="{16088070-7806-49C4-AED1-E1B1DA63D6E9}"
          KeyPath="yes"
          Directory="PhotosDir">
  <CreateFolder />
</Component>
```

3. Reference the `Component` in `Feature` element. You can use `ComponentRef` to do this:

```
<Feature Id="ProductFeature" Title="VirtualDirectoryInstaller"
Level="1">
  <ComponentGroupRef Id="ProductComponents" />
  <ComponentRef Id="cmpCssFolder"/>
  <ComponentRef Id="cmpScriptsFolder"/>
  <ComponentRef Id="cmpPhotosFolder" />
</Feature>
```

4. Now that we have the folder set up to be installed, register it as a virtual directory in the website by adding a `WebVirtualDir` element inside the `WebSite` element. Its `Directory` attribute should match `Id` of the `Directory` element:

```
<Component Id="cmpMyWebsite"
           Guid="{4073CF09-CE65-40D9-A0FA-1CE88B317E88}"
           KeyPath="yes">
  <iis:WebSite Id="website_MyWebsite"
               Description="MyWebsite"
               Directory="INSTALLFOLDER"
               ConfigureIfExists="yes">
    <iis:WebApplication Id="webapplication_MyWebsite"
                        Name="MyWebApplication"
                        WebAppPool="MyAppPool" />

    <iis:WebAddress Id="webaddress_MyWebsite"
                    Port="8080" />

    <iis:WebVirtualDir Id="webvirtualdir_MyWebsite"
                       Alias="Images"
                       Directory="PhotosDir" />
  </iis:WebSite>
</Component>
```

How it works...

Setting up the directory was nothing new. We added a `Directory` element so that it would be created on the end user's computer. In this example, since we aren't including any files in the folder, we placed `CreateFolder` within it to ensure that it is installed. Note that we used the `Component` element's `Directory` attribute to configure which `Directory` element our `CreateFolder` is associated with. The same purpose can be served by placing `Component` within `ComponentGroup` and using that element's `Directory` attribute.

To convert our normal `C:\Photos` directory to a virtual directory, we added a `WebVirtualDir` element inside our `WebSite` element. The `WebVirtualDir` element's `Alias` attribute will be the name of the folder shown in the IIS manager and can be different than the actual name of the folder. Here, we called it `Images`. Its `Directory` attribute points to our `PhotosDir Directory` element.

After running the installer, `Images` should now be displayed under the **MyWebsite** node. Notice that it has a shortcut-style arrow on it to distinguish it from the other two directories listed, as shown in the following screenshot:

Adding a web application to IIS

Inside a website, we can add two types of folders: virtual directories and web applications. Virtual directories simply map to folders outside our website's root. Web applications, on the other hand, are folders that can host entirely isolated modules. For example, we may develop a web application for a login page and another for a shopping cart. Their URLs might be `mysite.com/Login` and `mysite.com/ShoppingCart`. Each will get its own app domain to run in and could be completely oblivious to the other, with its own configuration, application pool, and worker process. However, to the end user, they will appear to be integrated parts of the same site.

Getting ready

To prepare for this recipe, perform the following steps:

1. Create a new setup project and name it `WebApplicationInstaller`.
2. Add `IIsExtension` to the project by right-clicking on the **References** node in **Solution Explorer** and going to **Add Reference...** | **WixIIsExtension.dll** | **Add** | **OK**.

3. Add the `IIsExtension` namespace to the `Wix` element:

```
<Wix xmlns="http://schemas.microsoft.com/wix/2006/wi"
xmlns:iis="http://schemas.microsoft.com/wix/IIsExtension">
```

4. Set up separate `Directory` elements for our website and the Web application. We will keep them under a common folder called `MyCompany`:

```
<Directory Id="TARGETDIR" Name="SourceDir">
  <Directory Id="ProgramFilesFolder">
    <Directory Id="CompanyFolder" Name="MyCompany">
      <Directory Id="MyWebsiteFolder" Name="MyWebsite" />
      <Directory Id="MyAppFolder" Name="MyApp" />
    </Directory>
  </Directory>
</Directory>
```

5. Add an HTML file called `Default.htm` to be displayed when the user navigates to our web application.

6. Add the `Component` and `File` elements to include `Default.htm` in the installer. Be sure to set the `Component` element's `Directory` attribute to `MyAppFolder`:

```
<Component Id="cmpWebAppDefaultHTM"
           Guid="{56F56AAB-F1E0-43A8-8023-30B566D1AE73}"
           KeyPath="yes"
           Directory="MyAppFolder">
  <File Source="Default.htm" />
</Component>
```

7. Include this Component element in our installer's feature:

```
<Feature Id="ProductFeature"
         Title="WebApplicationInstaller"
         Level="1">
  <ComponentGroupRef Id="ProductComponents" />
  <ComponentRef Id="cmpWebAppDefaultHTM" />
</Feature>
```

8. Add an app pool and website to the installer as described previously. The website will serve as the parent to our application. Use the following markup:

```
<ComponentGroup Id="ProductComponents"
                Directory="MyWebsiteFolder">
  <Component Id="cmpMyAppPool"
             Guid="{27D7BA04-706A-4755-9ACF-D026C6A7C1E9}"
             KeyPath="yes">
    <iis:WebAppPool Id="MyAppPool"
                    Name="MyWebsiteAppPool"
```

```
                              ManagedRuntimeVersion="v4.0"
                              ManagedPipelineMode="integrated"
                              Identity="applicationPoolIdentity" />
    </Component>

    <Component Id="cmpMyWebsite"
               Guid="{95565B4A-C24A-4F64-9644-DE64973DE6B3}"
               KeyPath="yes">
      <iis:WebSite Id="website_MyWebsite"
                   Description="MyWebsite"
                   ConfigureIfExists="yes"
                   Directory="MyWebsiteFolder">
        <iis:WebApplication Id="webapplication_MyWebsite"
                            Name="MyWebApplication"
                            WebAppPool="MyAppPool" />
        <iis:WebAddress Id="webaddress_MyWebsite"
                        Port="8080" />
      </iis:WebSite>
    </Component>
  </ComponentGroup>
```

How to do it...

Add a virtual directory to the website and then include a web application within it. The following steps will show you how to do it.

1. Within the `WebSite` element, add a `WebVirtualDir` element to create a virtual directory. Set its `Directory` attribute to point to `MyAppFolder`:

    ```
    <iis:WebSite ...>
      <iis:WebApplication ... />
      <iis:WebAddress ... />

      <iis:WebVirtualDir Id="webvirtualdir_MyApp"
                         Alias="MyApp"
                         Directory="MyAppFolder">

      </iis:WebVirtualDir>
    </iis:WebSite>
    ```

2. Inside `WebVirtualDir`, add a `WebApplication` element:

    ```
    <iis:WebVirtualDir ...>
      <iis:WebApplication Id="webapplication_MyApp"
                          Name="MyWebApplication"
                          WebAppPool="MyAppPool" />
    </iis:WebVirtualDir>
    ```

How it works...

We used the `WebApplication` element before when we nested it inside our `WebSite` element. In that case, it only sets the app pool for the website. However, when we place `WebApplication` inside `WebVirtualDir`, we're saying that this virtual directory hosts an application that can be separated by a process boundary from the parent website. In this example, we had the application use the same app pool as the website. However, we could have chosen a different app pool so that the application would run in its own isolated environment.

After installation, we'll see that our new web application, **MyApp**, is listed in the IIS manager under **MyWebsite**, as follows:

If we open **MyApp** in a browser, we can see that it shares the same root URL as our website, `http://localhost:8080`. However, our web application runs in the `/MyApp` subdirectory:

So, although it looks like a single, unified website to the end user, it's actually a website and an isolated application running within that site. Of course, our application is only serving a single HTML file, but it could easily host a full-fledged ASP.NET application.

Setting up a website to use SSL

Secure Sockets Layer (**SSL**) is a protocol that uses certificates and keys to encrypt data while it travels over a network. This way, private information is kept secret between two parties. WiX gives us both a way to install certificates to the keystores of the target machine and to associate one of those certificates with our website during installation to enable SSL.

In this recipe, we'll create a self-signed certificate and install it to the **Trusted Root Certification Authorities** and **Personal** keystores. We'll then install a website and bind it to the certificate. In a real-world scenario, you will have your certificate signed by a globally trusted certificate authority. However, for demonstration purposes, self-signing works best.

Getting ready

To prepare for this recipe, perform the following steps:

1. Create a new setup project and name it `SecureWebsiteInstaller`.

2. Add `IIsExtension` to the project by right-clicking on the **References** node in **Solution Explorer** and going to **Add Reference...** | **WixIIsExtension.dll** | **Add** | **OK**.

3. Add the `IIsExtension` namespace to the `Wix` element:

    ```
    <Wix xmlns="http://schemas.microsoft.com/wix/2006/wi"
    xmlns:iis="http://schemas.microsoft.com/wix/IIsExtension">
    ```

4. Add an application pool to IIS using the `WebAppPool` element, as discussed previously. Set `Id` to `MyAppPool`.

5. Add an HTML file called `Default.htm` to the project and include it in the installation using the `Component` and `File` elements.

6. We will need a certificate to bind to our website's listening port. The `makecert.exe` program from the Windows 8 SDK can be used to create a self-signed certificate. Download and install the SDK from `http://msdn.microsoft.com/en-us/windows/desktop/hh852363.aspx`. Then, open a Windows command prompt, navigate to the `C:\Program Files (x86)\Windows Kits\8.0\bin\x86` folder, and issue the following command:

    ```
    makecert -r -pe -n "CN=mywebsite.com" -sv "C:\MyCertAuthority.pvk"
    -sky exchange "C:\MyCertificate.cer"
    ```

7. You will be prompted twice to enter a password for the private key. Use `privatekey123` both times.

8. The previous command created a private key and a public certificate and saved them to C:\. Include both in a single password-protected PFX file using the pvk2pfx. exe program, which is also included with the Windows SDK. The -po argument protects the PFX file with a password. For this example, we'll set the password to mypfxpassword:

   pvk2pfx -po mypfxpassword -pvk "C:\MyCertAuthority.pvk" -spc "C:\ MyCertificate.cer" -pfx "C:\MyCertKeyPair.pfx"

9. You will be prompted for the private key that we set earlier. Enter privatekey123.

10. Copy the newly-created PFX file to your WiX project. We will include it in the installation as part of this recipe.

11. On the server that you'll be installing to, make sure that DNS is set up to route mywebsite.com to that machine's IP address. A DNS entry is required for SSL to work. Note that the **common name** (**CN**) that we set in the certificate is mywebsite. com to match the domain name we'll give to our website.

How to do it...

Install a PFX file using Certificate elements and then bind it to a website using the WebAddress element's Port, Header, and Secure attributes and a CertificateRef element. Follow these steps:

1. Inside the fragment that contains our components, add a Binary element that points to our MyCertKeyPair.pfx file:

```
<Fragment>
  <Binary Id="binary_MyCertKeyPairPFX"
          SourceFile="MyCertKeyPair.pfx" />

  <!--ComponentGroups, etc. go here-->
</Fragment>
```

2. Add a component with two Certificate elements inside it. The first element installs our PFX file in the Trusted Root Certification Authorities keystore on the end user's machine. The second element installs the same PFX file in the Personal keystore. Set the PFXPassword attribute to mypfxpassword since that's the phrase we used to protect the file with a password when we used the pvk2pfx program:

```
<ComponentGroup Id="ProductComponents"
                Directory="INSTALLFOLDER">

  <!--WebAppPool and Default.htm components omitted-->
```

```
<Component Id="cmpMyWebsite"
           Guid="{95565B4A-C24A-4F64-9644-DE64973DE6B3}"
           KeyPath="yes">
  <iis:Certificate Id="MyCertificateAuthority"
                   BinaryKey="binary_MyCertKeyPairPFX"
                   Name="MyCertificate"
                   StoreLocation="localMachine"
                   StoreName="root"
                   PFXPassword="password"/>

  <iis:Certificate Id="MyWebsiteCertificate"
                   BinaryKey="binary_MyCertKeyPairPFX"
                   Name="MyCertificate"
                   StoreLocation="localMachine"
                   StoreName="personal"
                   PFXPassword="mypfxpassword" />
</Component>
</ComponentGroup>
```

3. Within the same component, add a `WebSite` element with a child `WebApplication` and `WebAddress` element. Set the `WebAddress` element's `Port` attribute to `443`, its `Header` to `mywebsite.com` so that it matches our certificate's common name, and `Secure` to `yes`. Be sure that you added a DNS entry for `mywebsite.com` or updated your hosts file. Refer to the following snippet:

```
<iis:WebSite Id="website_MyWebsite"
             Description="MyWebsite"
             ConfigureIfExists="yes"
             Directory="INSTALLFOLDER">

  <iis:WebApplication Id="webapplication_MyWebsite"
                      Name="MyWebApplication"
                      WebAppPool="MyAppPool" />
  <iis:WebAddress Id="webaddress_MyWebsite"
                  Port="443"
                  Header="mywebsite.com"
                  Secure="yes" />
</iis:WebSite>
```

4. Add a `CertificateRef` element inside the `WebSite` element. Its `Id` attribute should point to the `Certificate` element that we placed in the personal store:

```
<iis:WebSite ...>

   <iis:WebApplication ... />
   <iis:WebAddress ... />

   <iis:CertificateRef Id="MyWebsiteCertificate"/>
</iis:WebSite>
```

How it works...

To make a website secure, we must bind a public certificate private key pair to its port. Our PFX is exactly that—a password-protected file containing both our CER and PVK file. The important requirement for the certificate is that it should have a common name that matches the hostname of our site. In this case, we used `mywebsite.com`, setting it in both the certificate and the `WebAddress` element's `Header` attribute. If the two do not match, we'll get an error that says the certificate was issued for a website with a different name, as shown in the following screenshot:

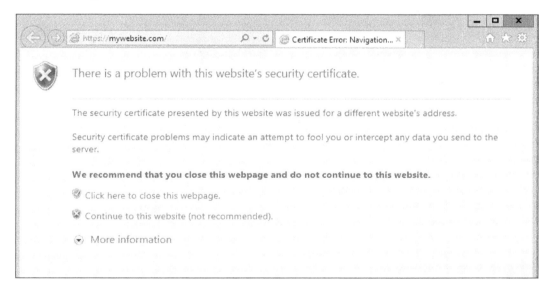

Beware, in IIS, there's a link labelled **Server Certificates** under the machine node:

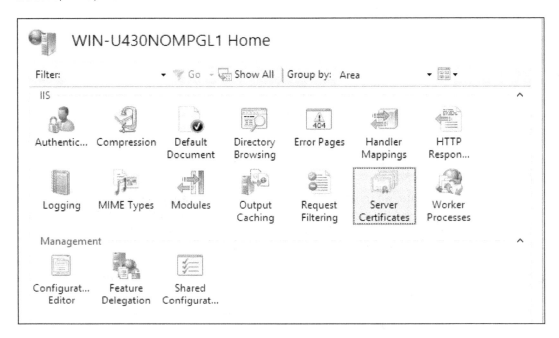

After double-clicking on it, you'll see an option to the right to create a self-signed certificate. I recommend you to not use this option since it doesn't give you a way to set the common name of the certificate. Instead, use the `makecert` program from the Windows SDK so that you can create a certificate with a common name that matches your site's address binding.

Once we created our PFX file, we referenced it in our installer using a `Binary` element. This included it within the MSI, but to install it into a particular keystore on the end user's computer, we used the `Certificate` element from `IIsExtension`. The first `Certificate` element adds it as a certificate authority in the Trusted Root Certification Authorities keystore. This way, the certificate that we install in the `Personal` keystore is trusted; it essentially trusts itself, which is fine for a `DEV` environment. If we only installed it in the Personal store, we'd see the following error when we visited the website:

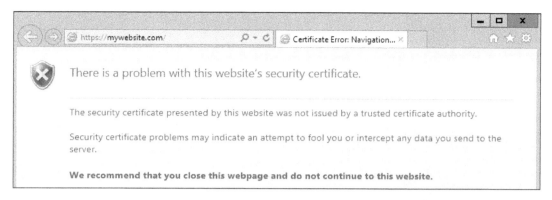

The final step was to associate the certificate in the Personal keystore with our website. So, we added a `WebSite` element inside the same component as the two `Certificate` elements and then set up a `WebAddress` element to use port `443`, have a `Header` of `mywebsite.com`, and `Secure` set to `yes`. Then, we added a `CertificateRef` element that points to our second `Certificate` element. That's enough to configure the SSL binding in IIS, as shown:

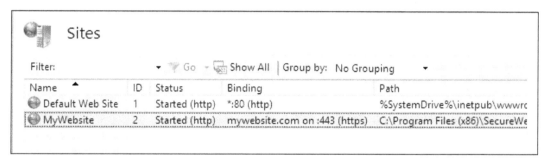

Now, when we navigate to `https://mywebsite.com`, and notice that we're using HTTPS and not HTTP, we get our `Default.htm` web page:

The website will now encrypt all requests and responses, ensuring that sensitive data is kept confidential.

11
Linking to the Web

In this chapter, we will cover the following:

- ▶ Adding a hyperlink control to a wizard dialog
- ▶ Opening an installed HTML file after a successful installation
- ▶ Launching a web page when a user uninstalls our software
- ▶ Installing a shortcut that opens a web page
- ▶ Updating programs and features to show a link to our company's website

Introduction

Often, the best place to put documentation, product information, and support is online. This way, we can keep the information current and the amount of documents that we load onto the end user's computer small. We just need a way to direct the users to the resources. With WiX, we can show hyperlinks, open a website automatically, and add shortcuts that link to a web page. Or, if we want to keep information offline, we can copy the HTML files locally and open them from there. The following recipes will explore how we can connect our installation with the Web.

Adding a hyperlink control to a wizard dialog

WiX contains a hyperlink control to create a link on a dialog. It was introduced in Windows Installer 5.0, which is preinstalled on Windows 7, Windows Server 2008 R2, and later versions of Windows. On older systems, such as Windows XP, if you try to run an install package that uses a hyperlink, you'll get an error. If you'd like to prevent users from installing your MSI when they don't have the required version of Windows Installer, then add 500 (which stands for version 5.0) to the `Package` element's `InstallerVersion` attribute, as follows:

```
<Package InstallerVersion="500"
         Compressed="yes"
         InstallScope="perMachine" />
```

In this recipe, we'll replace the default license text on the `WixUI_Minimal` wizard with a hyperlink to the GNU General Public License.

> If you create an RTF file in WordPad to be used as your license agreement and type the URL of a web page, WordPad will underline it and convert it to a hyperlink. However, Windows Installer will fail to display it correctly and it will not be clickable during installation. This is because the `ScrollableText` control that displays the RTF file does not support this behavior. The hyperlink control gives us a way to display a link.

Getting ready

To prepare for this recipe, perform the following steps:

1. Create a new setup project and name it `HyperlinkInstaller`.

2. Add `UIExtension` to the project by right-clicking on the **References** node in **Solution Explorer** and navigating to **Add Reference... | WixUIExtension.dll | Add | OK**.

3. Download the source code for the WiX toolset from `http://wix.codeplex.com/SourceControl/latest`.

4. Unzip the ZIP file and navigate within it to the `src\ext\UIExtension\wixlib` directory.

5. We'll be customizing the `WixUI_Minimal` wizard, so copy `WixUI_Minimal.wxs` from the `wixlib` directory to your setup project and rename it `CustomUI_Minimal.wxs`.

6. In `CustomUI_Minimal.wxs`, change the UI element to have the `Id` value of `CustomUI_Minimal`. This way it won't clash with the WXS file in the WiX toolset:

    ```
    <UI Id="CustomUI_Minimal">
    ```

7. In the same file, update `DialogRef` that has `Id` of `WelcomeEulaDlg` to use `HyperlinkWelcomeEulaDlg` instead:

    ```
    <DialogRef Id="HyperlinkWelcomeEulaDlg" />
    ```

8. Update the `Show` elements inside `InstallUISequence` to use `HyperlinkWelcomeEulaDlg` instead of `WelcomeEulaDlg`:

    ```
    <InstallUISequence>
      <Show Dialog="WelcomeDlg"
            Before="HyperlinkWelcomeEulaDlg">
        Installed AND PATCH
      </Show>
      <Show Dialog="HyperlinkWelcomeEulaDlg"
            Before="ProgressDlg">
        NOT Installed
      </Show>
    </InstallUISequence>
    ```

9. Copy `WelcomeEulaDlg.wxs` from the `wixlib` folder to your project and rename it `HyperlinkWelcomeEulaDlg.wxs`.

10. In `HyperlinkWelcomeEulaDlg.wxs`, update the top-level `Dialog` element to have `Id` of `HyperlinkWelcomeEulaDlg`.

11. In the same file, update the `Show` element inside `InstallUISequence` to use `HyperlinkWelcomeEulaDlg` for its `Dialog` attribute:

    ```
    <InstallUISequence>
      <Show Dialog="HyperlinkWelcomeEulaDlg"
            Before="ProgressDlg"
            Overridable="yes">
        NOT Installed
      </Show>
    </InstallUISequence>
    ```

12. In your `Product.wxs` file, add a `UIRef` element that points to `CustomUI_Minimal`:

    ```
    <UIRef Id="CustomUI_Minimal"/>
    ```

How to do it...

You can add a `Hyperlink` control that contains a `Text` element that specifies the URL to which you'd like to link. The following steps will show you how to do it:

1. The welcome screen of your `CustomUI_Minimal` wizard, which we've renamed `HyperlinkWelcomeEulaDlg`, contains a `ScrollableText` control to display the end user license agreement. Since we'll be replacing it with a hyperlink, remove it or comment it out:

   ```
   <!--<Control Id="LicenseText" Type="ScrollableText" X="130" Y="36"
   Width="226" Height="162" Sunken="yes" TabSkip="no">
     <Text SourceFile="!(wix.WixUILicenseRtf=$(var.licenseRtf))" />
   </Control>-->
   ```

2. Add a `Control` element that has a `Type` attribute of `Hyperlink`. Set its X, Y, `Width`, and `Height` attributes to the same values that the `ScrollableText` control has so that it will be positioned in the same spot on the dialog:

   ```
   <Control  Id="HyperlinkLicense"
             Type="Hyperlink"
             X="130"
             Y="36"
             Width="226"
             Height="162">
   </Control>
   ```

3. Inside that `Control` element, add a `Text` element that sets the target of the hyperlink. Its inner text, which we'll surround with CDATA tags, should take the form of an HTML anchor tag. In this example, we'll link to the GNU General Public License:

   ```
   <Control ...>
     <Text>
       <![CDATA[<a href="http://www.gnu.org/licenses/gpl.html">GNU
   General Public License</a>]]>
     </Text>
   </Control>
   ```

How it works...

Starting with Windows Installer 5.0, we have the ability to add a hyperlink to a WiX dialog. In this recipe, we replaced the `ScrollableText` control that displayed the end user license agreement with a hyperlink control that points to the web page of the GNU General Public License:

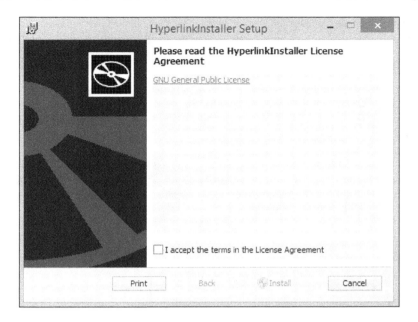

The `Hyperlink` control contains a `Text` element that specifies the target URL.
The `Text` element uses an HTML anchor tag with an `href` attribute to specify the
web page that should open:

```
<Text>
  <![CDATA[<a href="http://www.gnu.org/licenses/gpl.html">GNU General
Public License</a>]]>
</Text>
```

The `href` attribute can point to a web page, a file share, an absolute or relative path on the
computer, or a WiX property within square brackets. Although this is HTML, the markup that
you can use is limited. You cannot add other HTML styling or layout elements. When a user
launches our installer and clicks on the link, a browser will open and display the GNU website:

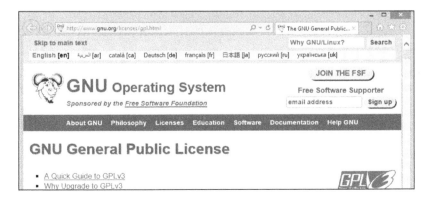

Opening an installed HTML file after a successful installation

Suppose we include a file called Changelog.html in our installer that outlines the recent changes to our software. We can then display this file as soon as the installation has finished, giving the user a quick guide as to what's new. The UtilExtension namespace contains a custom action called WixShellExec that can open an HTML file in the user's default browser.

Conveniently, each of the UI wizards that ship with the WiX toolset ends with a dialog that can optionally display a checkbox with a customizable label. We can control what happens when the user clicks the checkbox. In this recipe, we'll add the **Show Changelog** label and launch our HTML file when the user checks the box.

Getting ready

To prepare for this recipe, perform the following steps:

1. Create a new setup project and call it OpenHtmlDocumentInstaller.

2. Add UIExtension to the project by right-clicking on the **References** node in **Solution Explorer** and navigating to **Add Reference... | WixUIExtension.dll | Add | OK**.

3. Add one of the built-in wizards such as WixUI_Minimal to Product.wxs:

   ```
   <UIRef Id="WixUI_Minimal"/>
   ```

4. Now the checkbox will be displayed and its label will be set to **Show Changelog**, add a Property element called WIXUI_EXITDIALOGOPTIONALCHECKBOXTEXT, as follows:

   ```
   <Property Id="WIXUI_EXITDIALOGOPTIONALCHECKBOXTEXT"
           Value="Show Changelog" />
   ```

How to do it...

Use the WixShellExec custom action to open an HTML document after an installation, as shown in the following steps:

1. Add an HTML file called ChangeLog.html to the project and then include it in the installer with a Component and File element. Note that in this case we're adding Id to the File element. This will allow us to reference it directly later on. If you wish, you can add markup about fictitious changes to your software to the file with a few bullet points :

   ```
   <ComponentGroup Id="ProductComponents"
   ```

```
                      Directory="INSTALLFOLDER">
    <Component Id="cmpChangeLogHTML"
              Guid="{8B23C76B-F7D4-4030-8C46-1B5729E616B5}">
      <File Id="fileChangeLogHTML"
            Source="ChangeLog.html" />
    </Component>
</ComponentGroup>
```

2. Add `UtilExtension` to the project by right-clicking on the **References** node in **Solution Explorer** and navigating to **Add Reference... | WixUtilExtension.dll | Add | OK** so that we can access the `WixShellExec` custom action.

3. Add a property called `WixShellExecTarget` to your `Product.wxs` file. This sets up which file to open after the installation. Set its `Value` attribute to the `Id` of the `File` element of `ChangeLog`, preceded by a hash sign and surrounded by square brackets. During installation, this will be expanded to the file's path:

```
<Property Id="WixShellExecTarget"
          Value="[#fileChangeLogHTML]" />
```

4. Add a `CustomAction` element that has its `BinaryKey` attribute set to `WixCA`, its `DllEntry` attribute set to `WixShellExec`, and `Impersonate` set to yes:

```
<CustomAction Id="OpenChangeLog"
              BinaryKey="WixCA"
              DllEntry="WixShellExec"
              Impersonate="yes" />
```

5. Add the following `UI` and `Publish` elements so that the custom action is run at the end of the installation only if the checkbox is checked. The `Publish` element's `Value` attribute should match the ID of our `CustomAction` element. These can go somewhere inside your `Product.wxs` file:

```
<UI>
  <Publish Dialog="ExitDialog"
           Control="Finish"
           Event="DoAction"
           Value="OpenChangeLog">
WIXUI_EXITDIALOGOPTIONALCHECKBOX = 1 and NOT Installed
  </Publish>
</UI>
```

6. Run the installer and at the end, you'll see the following dialog:

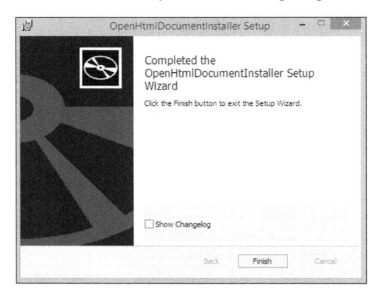

7. Check the box and click on **Finish** to see `ChangeLog`:

How it works...

The `WixShellExec` custom action from `UtilExtension` will open an HTML file for us in the end user's default browser. We added our `ChangeLog.html` file to the installer and then referenced it with a `Property` element named `WixShellExecTarget`. This sets up which file to open when the action is called.

Next, we added a `CustomAction` element that targets the `WixShellExec` method in the `WixCA` library, which is a part of `UtilExtension`:

```
<CustomAction Id="OpenChangeLog"
              BinaryKey="WixCA"
              DllEntry="WixShellExec"
              Impersonate="yes" />
```

All that was left was to tie this custom action to the **Finish** button on the final dialog, which we did by adding a `Publish` element that fired the `DoAction` event:

```
<Publish Dialog="ExitDialog"
         Control="Finish"
         Event="DoAction"
         Value="OpenChangeLog">
```

Note that we added a conditional statement inside the `Publish` element so that our action will be executed only if the checkbox is checked:

```
WIXUI_EXITDIALOGOPTIONALCHECKBOX = 1 and NOT Installed
```

The `NOT Installed` statement ensures that our action will run only during an installation and not during a repair, upgrade, or uninstallation.

There's more...

If you'd rather force the change log to open without asking the user to check a box, then we can simply remove the `WIXUI_EXITDIALOGOPTIONALCHECKBOXTEXT` property, omit steps 5–7, and instead add our custom action to `InstallExecuteSequence`, as follows:

```
<InstallExecuteSequence>
  <Custom Action="OpenChangeLog"
          After="InstallFinalize">NOT Installed</Custom>
</InstallExecuteSequence>
```

Now, the checkbox won't be displayed at all and our `ChangeLog.html` file will open at the end of the installation. In fact, the user won't even have to click on the **Finish** button.

Starting with Windows Installer 5.0, there is a control event called `MsiLaunchApp` that does the same thing as the `WixShellExec` custom action. You can use it to open an HTML file when the user clicks a button, just like we did in this recipe. You can use this if you're building your own dialogs from scratch. You can find more information at http://msdn.microsoft.com/en-us/library/windows/ desktop/dd408008(v=vs.85).aspx.

Since Windows Installer 5.0 is required, this will only work on Windows 7, Windows Server 2008 R2 and newer operating systems. There is no redistributable for Windows Installer 5.0, so you can't install it on, say, Windows XP.

Launching a web page when a user uninstalls our software

When a user uninstalls our software, often we want to know why. In this recipe, we'll see how to open a web page in `surveymonkey.com` after an uninstallation. We can use this site to build a survey that asks the user why they're removing the software.

Getting ready

To prepare for this recipe, perform the following steps:

1. Create a new setup project and call it `OpenWebPageAfterUninstallInstaller`.

2. We have to add at least one file to our installer for the installation to complete successfully. Add a file called `Sample.txt` to the project and add the `Component` and `File` elements to include it in the installation:

```
<ComponentGroup Id="ProductComponents"
                Directory="INSTALLFOLDER">
  <Component Id="cmpSampleTXT"
             Guid="{71C66E47-B398-4F06-98C9-4143495772A4}">
    <File Source="Sample.txt" />
  </Component>
</ComponentGroup>
```

How to do it...

Schedule the `WixShellExec` custom action to run after `InstallFinalize` in `InstallExecuteSequence`, but only during an uninstallation. The following steps will show how to open the web page:

1. Add `UtilExtension` to the project by right-clicking on the **References** node in **Solution Explorer** and navigating to **Add Reference... | WixUtilExtension.dll | Add | OK**.

2. In your `Product.wxs` file, add a `Property` element with `Id` of `WixShellExecTarget` and `Value` set to the URL of the website to open:

```
<Property Id="WixShellExecTarget"
          Value="https://www.surveymonkey.com" />
```

3. Add a `CustomAction` element with `BinaryKey` set to `WixCA`, `DllEntry` set to `WixShellExec`, and `Impersonate` set to `yes`:

```
<CustomAction Id="OpenWebPage"
              BinaryKey="WixCA"
```

```
            DllEntry="WixShellExec"
            Impersonate="yes" />
```

4. Add the custom action to `InstallExecuteSequence` by using a `Custom` element. Its `Action` attribute should match the `Id` of the `CustomAction` element and its `After` attribute should be set to `InstallFinalize`. Inside the `Custom` element, add the conditional statement `REMOVE ~= ALL` so that the action will only be run during an uninstallation:

```
<InstallExecuteSequence>
  <Custom Action="OpenWebPage" After="InstallFinalize">
    REMOVE ~= "ALL"
  </Custom>
</InstallExecuteSequence>
```

How it works...

The `WixShellExec` custom action opens a web page that we have specified with the `WixShellExecTarget` property. We scheduled this action to run during `InstallExecuteSequence`. To ensure that the web page will only open when we want it to, we check the value of the `REMOVE` property. It has a value of `ALL` during a complete uninstallation. The tilde makes the verification case insensitive.

Installing a shortcut that opens a web page

In the previous recipes, we added a shortcut to our software on the **Start** menu. We can also add a shortcut to a web page—perhaps one where the user can find information about other related products. It's a great way to keep the resources front and center. In this recipe, we'll add a shortcut to the **Start** menu that opens the website, `http://www.packtpub.com`.

Getting ready

To prepare for this recipe, create a new setup project and name it `WebPageShortcutInstaller`.

How to do it...

Include an `InternetShortcut` element from `UtilExtension` to create a shortcut to a website, as shown in the following steps:

1. Add `UtilExtension` to the project by right-clicking on the **References** node in **Solution Explorer** and navigating to **Add Reference... | WixUtilExtension.dll | Add | OK**.

2. Add the `util` namespace to the `Wix` element:

```
<Wix xmlns="http://schemas.microsoft.com/wix/2006/wi"
xmlns:util="http://schemas.microsoft.com/wix/UtilExtension">
```

3. Use the `Directory` elements to add a new folder to the Windows **Start** menu. This is where our shortcut will go. In this example, we'll add a folder called `My Software`:

```
<Directory Id="TARGETDIR" Name="SourceDir">
  <Directory Id="ProgramFilesFolder">
    <Directory Id="INSTALLFOLDER"
               Name="My Software" />
  </Directory>
  <Directory Id="ProgramMenuFolder">
    <Directory Id="MyStartMenuFolder"
               Name="My Software" />
  </Directory>
</Directory>
```

4. Add `Component` that contains an `InternetShortcut` element from the `util` namespace. This will define where to place the shortcut and to which URL it will point:

```
<ComponentGroup Id="ProductComponents"
                Directory="INSTALLFOLDER">
  <Component Id="cmpWebPageShortcut"
             Guid="{5A1DF50C-F232-4EA5-9178-B371EE7E1375}">
    <util:InternetShortcut Id="shortcutWebPage"
                           Directory="MyStartMenuFolder"
                           Name="See Other Products"
                           Target="https://www.packtpub.com"
                           Type="url" />
  </Component>
</ComponentGroup>
```

5. Add a `RemoveFolder` element to the same component so that our **Start** menu folder will be removed during an uninstall and add a `RegistryValue` element to serve as the component's `KeyPath` attribute:

```
<Component ...>
  <util:InternetShortcut .../>

  <RemoveFolder Id="removeStartMenuFolder"
                Directory="MyStartMenuFolder"
                On="uninstall" />
  <RegistryValue Root="HKCU"
                 Key="Software\MyCompany\MySoftware"
```

```
                           Name="installed"
                           Type="integer"
                           Value="1"
                           KeyPath="yes" />

    </Component>
```

How it works...

Although you can place a shortcut anywhere, we added it to the Windows **Start** menu in this recipe. The `UtilExtension` namespace gives us an element called `InternetShortcut` that will create a specialized shortcut that can open a web page, as shown in the following screenshot:

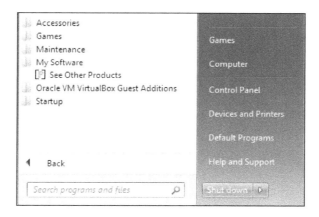

The `InternetShortcut` element's `Directory` attribute specifies where the shortcut will go. Its `Name` attribute is what will be displayed to the end user. `Target` sets the URL to navigate to and `Type` declares that the target is a URL:

```
    <util:InternetShortcut Id="shortcutWebPage"
                           Directory="MyStartMenuFolder"
                           Name="See Other Products"
                           Target="https://www.packtpub.com"
                           Type="url" />
```

Since we installed a new folder within the Windows **Start** menu, we must add a `RemoveFolder` and `RegistryValue` element. This is standard procedure when adding a folder to the **Start** menu, regardless of whether it includes `InternetShortcut`. They ensure that the folder is removed during an uninstall and we have something to serve as `KeyPath` for `Component`. After running the setup, the shortcut will be created and, when it is clicked, it will open our web page in the end user's default browser.

Updating programs and features to show a link to our company's website

We want to give a user every opportunity to get the most up-to-date information about our software. **Programs and Features**, which is where users can remove software from their system, is one place they might look for information. With WiX, we can customize how our software is displayed there and provide links to our company's website, a support page, and a page where users can find the latest downloads.

In this recipe, we will add three web page links for our software on the **Programs and Features** screen. Here is the end result:

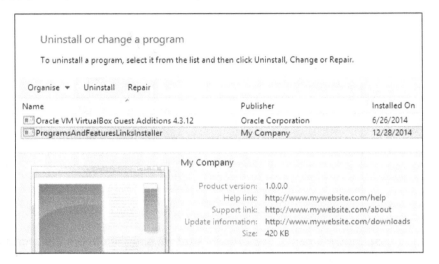

Getting ready

To prepare for this recipe, perform the following steps:

1. Create a new setup project and call it `ProgramsAndFeaturesLinksInstaller`.

2. Add a text file to the project and name it `Sample.txt` so that our installer has something to install. Add a `Component` element and a `File` element to include the file in the installer:

```
<ComponentGroup Id="ProductComponents"
                Directory="INSTALLFOLDER">
  <Component Id="cmpSampleTXT"
             Guid="{8E43E291-5F2F-4B62-B13E-E39DF145318D}">
    <File Source="Sample.txt" />
  </Component>
</ComponentGroup>
```

How to do it...

Add the `Property` elements that define the links to be displayed in **Programs and Features**, as shown in the following steps:

1. In your `Product.wxs` file, add the `Property` elements with the `Id` attributes of `ARPURLINFOABOUT`, `ARPHELPLINK`, and `ARPURLUPDATEINFO`. The first points to a page where the user can find more information about our company or software. The second points to a page where the user can find support information. The third points to a page where they can find the most up-to-date downloadable files for the software:

```
<Property Id="ARPURLINFOABOUT"
          Value="http://www.mywebsite.com/about" />
<Property Id="ARPHELPLINK"
          Value="http://www.mywebsite.com/help" />
<Property Id="ARPURLUPDATEINFO"
          Value="http://www.mywebsite.com/downloads" />
```

2. When the installation has finished, navigate to **Programs and Features** and select our application from the list of installed software. At the bottom of the screen, you'll see the three URLs that we have set.

How it works...

After installation, the `ARPURLINFOABOUT`, `ARPHELPLINK`, and `ARPURLUPDATEINFO` properties are stored in the Windows registry under `HKEY_LOCAL_MACHINE\SOFTWARE\Microsoft\Windows\CurrentVersion\Uninstall`. This is where all the data to display entries in **Programs and Features** is stored.

If you're interested in learning about other properties that affect how your software is shown in **Programs and Features**, such as how to change the icon that's displayed, go to `http://msdn.microsoft.com/en-us/library/aa368032(v=vs.85).aspx`.

12
Installing SQL Server Databases

In this chapter, we will cover the following topics:

- ▸ Installing a SQL Server instance with a bootstrapper
- ▸ Adding a database to a SQL Server instance
- ▸ Creating a table within a SQL Server database
- ▸ Inserting data into a database table
- ▸ Creating an ODBC data source for a SQL Server instance

Introduction

Data is vital to most applications. So, it's likely that you'll want to set up a database at installation time to store data. The WiX Toolset gives us a mechanism to add a new instance of SQL Server and then add databases, table definitions, and data to it. In this chapter, we'll cover these common tasks and also touch upon how to set up an ODBC data source, which gives a standardized way for applications of various types to connect to the database.

Installing a SQL Server instance with a bootstrapper

Unless you're sure that an instance of SQL Server is already installed on the end user's computer, you'll probably want to install it yourself. A bootstrapper can check for the existence of SQL Server and install it only if it isn't there, saving you the guesswork. In this recipe, we will create a bootstrapper that will install SQL Server 2014 Express. This is a free database offered by Microsoft.

How to do it...

Add `PackageGroup` for SQL Server 2014 Express to a bootstrapper project, as shown in the following steps:

1. Create a new bootstrapper project and call it `SqlServerBootstrapper`.

2. Add the `UtilExtension` namespace to the project by right-clicking on the **References** node in **Solution Explorer** and selecting **OK** after navigating to **Add Reference... | Browse | WixUtilExtension.dll | Add**.

3. Add `NetFxExtension` to the project by right-clicking on the **References** node in **Solution Explorer** and selecting **OK** after navigating to **Add Reference... | Browse | WixNetFxExtension.dll | Add**.

4. SQL Server 2014 Express has a dependency on either .NET 3.5 or .NET 4. We can get .NET 4 from `NetFxExtension` by opening our bootstrapper project's `Bundle.wxs` file and adding a `PackageGroupRef` element with an `Id` attribute of `NetFx40Redist`. Update the `Chain` element as follows:

   ```
   <Chain>
     <PackageGroupRef Id="NetFx40Redist"/>
   </Chain>
   ```

5. To keep our SQL Server markup separated, we'll add a new WXS file for it. Right-click on the project and select **Installer File** after navigating to **Add | New Item...** and then set its name to `SqlServerPackageGroup.wxs`:

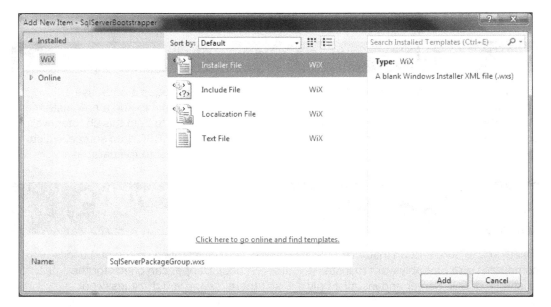

6. Download the 64-bit installer for SQL Server 2014 Express from `http://
download.microsoft.com/download/E/A/E/EAE6F7FC-767A-4038-A954-
49B8B05D04EB/Express%2064BIT/SQLEXPR_x64_ENU.exe`. If you prefer the
32-bit version, it can be found at `http://download.microsoft.com/download/
E/A/E/EAE6F7FC-767A-4038-A954-49B8B05D04EB/Express%2032BIT/
SQLEXPR_x86_ENU.exe`.

7. Copy the SQL Server installer, `SQLEXPR_x64_ENU.exe`, to the bootstrapper project's
directory so that it sits next to our `SqlServerPackageGroup.wxs` file.

8. Update `SqlServerPackageGroup.wxs` with the following markup:

```xml
<?xml version="1.0" encoding="UTF-8"?>
<Wix xmlns="http://schemas.microsoft.com/wix/2006/wi"
xmlns:util="http://schemas.microsoft.com/wix/UtilExtension">

  <!--Instance name is limited to 16 characters-->
  <?define SqlInstanceName=MySqlInstance?>

  <?define SqlInstallCommand=/ACTION=Install /Q /
IACCEPTSQLSERVERLICENSETERMS /FEATURES=SQLEngine /
INSTANCENAME=$(var.SqlInstanceName) /SQLSYSADMINACCOUNTS=BUILTIN\
Administrators /SECURITYMODE=SQL /SAPWD=password123 ?>

  <?define SqlUninstallCommand=/ACTION=Uninstall /Q /
FEATURES=SQLEngine /INSTANCENAME=$(var.SqlInstanceName) ?>

  <?define SqlRepairCommand=/ACTION=Repair /Q /FEATURES=SQLEngine
/INSTANCENAME=$(var.SqlInstanceName) ?>

  <Fragment>
    <util:RegistrySearch Id="regsearchSqlInstanceFound"
                         Root="HKLM"
                         Key="SOFTWARE\Microsoft\Microsoft SQL
Server\Instance Names\SQL"
                         Value="$(var.SqlInstanceName)"
                         Result="exists"
                         Variable="SqlInstanceFound"/>

    <PackageGroup Id="SqlServerPackageGroup">
      <ExePackage SourceFile="SQLEXPR_x64_ENU.exe"
                  DetectCondition="SqlInstanceFound"
                  InstallCommand="$(var.SqlInstallCommand)"
                  UninstallCommand="$(var.SqlUninstallCommand)"
                  RepairCommand="$(var.SqlRepairCommand)" />
    </PackageGroup>
  </Fragment>
</Wix>
```

9. In `Bundle.wxs`, reference `PackageGroup` that we just defined using a `PackageGroupRef` element:

```
<Chain>
  <PackageGroupRef Id="NetFx40Redist"/>
  <PackageGroupRef Id="SqlServerPackageGroup"/>
</Chain>
```

10. Build and run the bootstrapper to verify that it installs SQL Server 2014 Express.

How it works...

SQL Server 2014 Express is available in a few different packages, such as bundled with **SQL Server Management Studio** (**SSMS**) or as a standalone installation. In this case, we went with the standalone option. However, you may want to install SSMS too during development so that you can check the databases and tables that we'll be adding in the next few recipes.

The 64-bit SQL Server Express standalone installer is called `SQLEXPR_x64_ENU.exe`. It relies on the .NET 3.5 or .NET 4 Framework. `NetFxExtension` can install .NET 4 for us if we add `PackageGroupRef` that points to `NetFx40Redist`:

```
<Chain>
  <PackageGroupRef Id="NetFx40Redist"/>
</Chain>
```

With this in place, the .NET Framework will be installed prior to SQL Server Express, but only if it's missing. Next, we added the SQL Server Express installer to our project and referenced it with an `ExePackage` element. During compilation, this file will be compressed into our bootstrapper executable.

Our bootstrapper sends command-line arguments to the SQL Server installation package to configure parameters during the installation, uninstallation and repair processes. Preprocessor variables are a convenient way to keep our long command-line arguments in one place. Note that we have one of these just to store the name of our SQL Server instance since it happens to be used in several places. Also note that the instance name has a maximum limit of 16 characters—just a limitation of SQL Server. Consider the following code snippet:

```
<?define SqlInstanceName=MySqlInstance?>


<?define SqlInstallCommand=/ACTION=Install /Q /
IACCEPTSQLSERVERLICENSETERMS /FEATURES=SQLEngine /INSTANCENAME=$(var.
SqlInstanceName) /SQLSYSADMINACCOUNTS=BUILTIN\Administrators /
SECURITYMODE=SQL /SAPWD=password123 ?>
```

```
<?define SqlUninstallCommand=/ACTION=Uninstall /Q /FEATURES=SQLEngine /
INSTANCENAME=$(var.SqlInstanceName) ?>
```

```
<?define SqlRepairCommand=/ACTION=Repair /Q /FEATURES=SQLEngine /
INSTANCENAME=$(var.SqlInstanceName) ?>
```

After defining these preprocessor variables, we match them up with attributes on the `ExePackage` element:

```
<PackageGroup Id="SqlServerPackageGroup">
  <ExePackage SourceFile="SQLEXPR_x64_ENU.exe"
              DetectCondition="SqlInstanceFound"
              InstallCommand="$(var.SqlInstallCommand)"
              UninstallCommand="$(var.SqlUninstallCommand)"
              RepairCommand="$(var.SqlRepairCommand)" />
</PackageGroup>
```

The `DetectCondition` attribute works a bit differently. It figures out whether the package is already installed, which helps the bootstrapper decide which command—install, uninstall, or repair—to run. It points to a variable defined by a `RegistrySearch` element that we've included in the same fragment:

```
<util:RegistrySearch Id="regsearchSqlInstanceFound"
                     Root="HKLM"
                     Key="SOFTWARE\Microsoft\Microsoft SQL Server\
Instance Names\SQL"
                     Value="$(var.SqlInstanceName)"
                     Result="exists"
                     Variable="SqlInstanceFound"/>
```

This will check the Windows registry whenever the bootstrapper is run to see whether our named SQL instance is there. If it is, a variable called `SqlInstanceFound` is set and that's what we will reference with the `DetectCondition` attribute.

The final step was to add `PackageGroupRef` inside the `Chain` element so that SQL Server Express will be installed after the .NET Framework:

```
<Chain>
  <PackageGroupRef Id="NetFx40Redist"/>
  <PackageGroupRef Id="SqlServerPackageGroup"/>
</Chain>
```

Adding a database to a SQL Server instance

Once we have an instance of SQL Server running on the end user's computer, the next step is to add a database to it. This will give us a place to store our application's data. With WiX, we can define a new database in a declarative style rather than with an external SQL script.

Getting ready

Create a new setup project and name it `NewDatabaseInstaller`.

How to do it...

The following steps show how to create a new database with the `SqlDatabase` element:

1. Add `SqlExtension` to the project by right-clicking on the **References** node in **Solution Explorer** and selecting **OK** after navigating to **Add Reference... | Browse | WixSqlExtension.dll | Add**.

2. Add the `SqlExtension` namespace to the `Wix` element:

   ```
   <Wix xmlns="http://schemas.microsoft.com/wix/2006/wi"
   xmlns:sql="http://schemas.microsoft.com/wix/SqlExtension">
   ```

3. Add a `Component` element that has `KeyPath` set to `yes`:

   ```
   <ComponentGroup Id="ProductComponents"
                   Directory="INSTALLFOLDER">
     <Component Id="cmpSqlDatabase"
                Guid="{F950605D-AA59-43E6-AB19-9452F6BEC649}"
                KeyPath="yes">
     </Component>
   </ComponentGroup>
   ```

4. Inside of it, include a `SqlDatabase` element that will define the database to add to an existing instance of SQL Server. The following creates a database called `MyDatabase` within a SQL Server instance called `MySqlInstance` that resides on the end user's computer:

   ```
   <ComponentGroup Id="ProductComponents"
                   Directory="INSTALLFOLDER">
     <Component Id="cmpSqlDatabase"
                Guid="{F950605D-AA59-43E6-AB19-9452F6BEC649}"
                KeyPath="yes">
       <sql:SqlDatabase Id="sqlDatabase_MyDatabase"
   ```

```
                          Server="[ComputerName]"
                          Instance="MySqlInstance"
                          Database="MyDatabase"
                          CreateOnInstall="yes"
                          DropOnUninstall="yes"
                          ContinueOnError="yes" />
       </Component>
     </ComponentGroup>
```

5. Run the installer and verify that the database was created. You can use SQL Server Management Studio to check this.

How it works...

`SqlExtension` from the WiX Toolset gives us a new element called `SqlDatabase` that will add a database to an instance of SQL Server. In this example, we're assuming that there's a named instance called `MySqlInstance` installed on the end user's computer. Of course, we could install it ourselves using a bootstrapper. The `ComputerName` property used in the `Server` attribute will be expanded to the name of the computer. The `Database` attribute sets up what to call our new database. Here, we called it `MyDatabase`.

With the `CreateOnInstall` and `DropOnUninstall` attributes, we were able to create the database during installation and remove it during an uninstall. If the database already exists, no action will be taken. The `ContinueOnError` attribute is set to yes to ensure that if there is an error while performing these actions, the installer will be able to continue. It's important not to get stuck on a SQL error, especially during the uninstallation since doing so would prevent the user from removing our software. Unfortunately, there isn't a way to set `ContinueOnError` to `no` and have it only affect installation.

Creating a table within a SQL Server database

After creating a database on the end user's computer, you'll want to define its schema by adding table definitions. WiX gives us a way to execute `CREATE TABLE` statements within the database that we're installing. In this recipe, we will add a table definition with a few basic fields.

Getting ready

Create a new setup project and name it `NewTableInstaller`.

How to do it...

To create a table, add a `SqlString` element that specifies the `CREATE TABLE` SQL statement:

1. Add `SqlExtension` to the project by right-clicking on the **References** node in **Solution Explorer** and selecting **OK** after navigating to **Add Reference... | Browse | WixSqlExtension.dll | Add**.

2. Add the `SqlExtension` namespace to the `Wix` element:

```
<Wix xmlns="http://schemas.microsoft.com/wix/2006/wi"
xmlns:sql="http://schemas.microsoft.com/wix/SqlExtension">
```

3. Add a `Component` that has its `KeyPath` attribute set to `yes`. It should contain a `SqlDatabase` element so that a database is set up for us to add a table to it:

```
<ComponentGroup Id="ProductComponents"
                Directory="INSTALLFOLDER">
  <Component Id="cmpSqlTable"
             Guid="{AB80A310-792B-40FF-8437-07BEAF75BFD5}"
             KeyPath="yes">
    <sql:SqlDatabase Id="sqlDatabase_MyDatabase"
                     Server="[ComputerName]"
                     Instance="MySqlInstance"
                     Database="MyDatabase"
                     CreateOnInstall="yes"
                     DropOnUninstall="yes"
                     ContinueOnError="yes">

    </sql:SqlDatabase>
  </Component>
</ComponentGroup>
```

4. Inside the `SqlDatabase` element, add a `SqlString` element that sets the SQL statement to `run`. The following markup will add a table to the `SqlDatabase` that it's nested under:

```
<sql:SqlDatabase ..>
  <sql:SqlString
    Id="sqlString_CreateTable"
    ExecuteOnInstall="yes"
    ContinueOnError="yes"
    SQL="IF NOT (EXISTS (SELECT *
         FROM INFORMATION_SCHEMA.TABLES
         WHERE TABLE_SCHEMA = 'dbo'
           AND TABLE_NAME = 'MyTable'))
         BEGIN
```

```
              CREATE TABLE MyTable (
                Id INT PRIMARY KEY IDENTITY,
                Name NVARCHAR(50) NOT NULL,
                Timestamp DATETIME DEFAULT CURRENT_TIMESTAMP)
            END"
        />
</sql:SqlDatabase>
```

5. Run the installer and verify that a table called `MyTable` is added to `MyDatabase`.

How it works...

After we've added a database using the `SqlDatabase` element of `SqlExtension`, we can execute SQL statements against it, including one to create a table. To do this, we nest a `SqlString` element within `SqlDatabase`. `SqlString` specifies a SQL attribute that defines the statement to run. As we've done here, the value of the SQL attribute can span multiple lines:

```
SQL="IF NOT (EXISTS (SELECT *
      FROM INFORMATION_SCHEMA.TABLES
      WHERE TABLE_SCHEMA = 'dbo'
        AND TABLE_NAME = 'MyTable'))
    BEGIN
      CREATE TABLE MyTable (
        Id INT PRIMARY KEY IDENTITY,
        Name NVARCHAR(50) NOT NULL,
        Timestamp DATETIME DEFAULT CURRENT_TIMESTAMP)
    END"
```

The `ExecuteOnInstall` attribute causes the statement to run only during an installation. With what we have so far, the database is not removed during an uninstallation process. We could have added a second `SqlString` element with its `ExecuteOnUninstall` attribute set to `yes` and its SQL attribute defined as a `DROP TABLE` statement. However, since the entire database is going to be dropped during the uninstallation process, there's no need.

To verify that the table is created, we can use SQL Server Management Studio to open the database and check whether our table is listed:

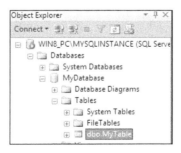

Inserting data into a database table

During the installation, you may decide to populate your database tables with some seed data. For example, you may have a list of U.S. states in which you do business that you'd like to add as static data. In this recipe, we will create a database, add a table to it, and then insert new rows into that table.

Getting ready

Create a new setup project and call it `InsertingDataInstaller`.

How to do it...

Include an `INSERT` statements in a `SqlScript` element to add rows of data to a database. The following steps show how to do it.

1. Add `SqlExtension` to the project by right-clicking on the **References** node in **Solution Explorer** and selecting **OK** after navigating to **Add Reference... | Browse | WixSqlExtension.dll | Add**.

2. Add the `SqlExtension` namespace to the `Wix` element:

   ```
   <Wix xmlns="http://schemas.microsoft.com/wix/2006/wi"
   xmlns:sql="http://schemas.microsoft.com/wix/SqlExtension">
   ```

3. We're going to store all our SQL commands in a file. So, use Notepad to create a file called `install_data.sql` and add the following statements to it:

   ```
   IF NOT (EXISTS (SELECT *
     FROM INFORMATION_SCHEMA.TABLES
     WHERE TABLE_SCHEMA = 'dbo'
       AND TABLE_NAME = 'States'))
   BEGIN
     CREATE TABLE States (
       Id INT PRIMARY KEY IDENTITY,
       Name NVARCHAR(20) NOT NULL);

     INSERT INTO [MyDatabase].[dbo].[States] (Name)
     VALUES (N'Alabama')
   END
   ```

4. Add this file to your setup project. You can drag it from the Windows Explorer to the Visual Studio Solution explorer. Don't create it directly in Visual Studio since there's a chance that invalid, invisible characters could be introduced.

5. Add a `Binary` element either inside of the `Product` element or the `Fragment` element that contains `ComponentGroup`. Its `SourceFile` attribute should point to our `install_data.sql` file:

```
<Binary Id="install_dataSQL"
        SourceFile="install_data.sql" />
```

6. Add a `Component` element with its `KeyPath` attribute set to `yes` and a `SqlDatabase` element nested inside of it. This will create the database that we will execute the SQL statements against:

```
<ComponentGroup Id="ProductComponents"
                Directory="INSTALLFOLDER">
  <Component Id="cmpInsertData"
             Guid="{A80B13D5-060C-4F95-84F0-7414AFE75F9B}"
KeyPath="yes">
    <sql:SqlDatabase Id="sqlDatabase_MyDatabase"
                     Server="[ComputerName]"
                     Instance="MySqlInstance"
                     Database="MyDatabase"
                     CreateOnInstall="yes"
                     DropOnUninstall="yes"
                     ContinueOnError="yes">
    </sql:SqlDatabase>
  </Component>
</ComponentGroup>
```

7. Within `SqlDatabase`, add a `SqlScript` element that references the `Binary` element we've defined for our `install_data.sql` file. Set its `ExecuteOnInstall` attribute to `yes`:

```
<sql:SqlDatabase ..>
  <sql:SqlScript Id="sqlScript_InsertData"
                 BinaryKey="install_dataSQL"
                 ExecuteOnInstall="yes"
                 ContinueOnError="yes" />
</sql:SqlDatabase>
```

8. Run the installer and verify that a row of data is added to `MyTable` in `MyDatabase`.

How it works...

Although we can use `SqlString` elements to execute `INSERT` statements against a database, it might involve many such elements. Instead, we can place all of our SQL into a separate file and reference it with a `Binary` element. Our `install_data.sql` file included the `CREATE TABLE` and `INSERT` statements so that the table is added and then populated. This also guarantees that the statements are run in the correct order.

When we nest `SqlScript` within a `SqlDatabase` element, the SQL statements it points to are executed against that database. The `BinaryKey` attribute identifies the `Binary` element to use and by setting `ExecuteOnInstall` to `yes`, the script will only run during the installation.

In this example, we didn't handle the uninstallation process explicitly. For example, we could have added another `SqlScript` with its `ExecuteOnUninstall` attribute set to `yes` to remove rows from the database or drop the table during the uninstallation process. However, since the `SqlDatabase` element will drop the entire database anyway, this step was not needed.

After running the installer, we can use SQL Server Management Studio to verify that a row was added to our database table:

Creating an ODBC data source for a SQL Server instance

Microsoft Open Database Connectivity (**ODBC**) is a long-standing and established API for connecting to a database. Although there are alternative .NET-specific libraries, such as Entity Framework, ODBC is more general purpose and fits well into an environment where a variety of languages and technology stacks are used.

Many languages have libraries that can take advantage of ODBC. For example, C# can use either ADO.NET or the classes under the `System.Data.Odbc` namespace to connect to an ODBC data source. In this recipe, we will set up a data source to connect to a SQL Server instance called `MySqlInstance`.

Getting ready

Create a new setup project and call it `OdbcDataSourceInstaller`.

How to do it...

Using the `ODBCDataSource` element, create a data source for SQL Server, as shown in the following steps:

1. Add a component to the project that will contain our ODBC data source:

```
<ComponentGroup Id="ProductComponents"
                Directory="INSTALLFOLDER">
  <Component Id="cmpOdbcDataSource"
             Guid="{B7D13BCD-A34C-4575-AE1E-4BA7D6A27D6C}">

  </Component>
</ComponentGroup>
```

2. Within this component, add an `ODBCDataSource` element that has its `DriverName` attribute set to SQL Server, its `Registration` attribute set to machine, and its `KeyPath` attribute set to `yes`. We can choose any name for it as long as it hasn't already been used by another ODBC data source:

```
<Component ...>
  <ODBCDataSource Id="OdbcDataSource_MySqlDataSource"
                  DriverName="SQL Server"
                  Registration="machine"
                  KeyPath="yes"
                  Name="MySqlDataSource">
  </ODBCDataSource>
</Component>
```

3. Within the `ODBCDataSource` element, add the `Property` elements to define other attributes of the ODBC data source, such as the SQL Server instance to connect to, the default database to use, and whether to use Windows authentication:

```
<ODBCDataSource ...>
  <Property Id="Server"
            Value="[ComputerName]\MySqlInstance" />
  <Property Id="Database"
            Value="master" />
  <Property Id="Description"
            Value="A description about my ODBC data source" />
```

```
        <Property Id="Trusted_Connection"
                Value="yes" />
    </ODBCDataSource>
```

4. Run the installer and verify that the data source was created. In Windows 8.1, you can navigate to **Control Panel | Administrative Tools | ODBC Data Sources (32-bit) | System DSN**. You can also type `odbcad32` in the **Run** window.

How it works...

The `ODBCDataSource` element will create a new data source using the specified driver. There are many drivers that come preinstalled on Windows 8, such as for Oracle, Microsoft Access, and SQL Server. You can open the **ODBC Data Sources Administrative Tools** window to find the names of others. For us, it's SQL Server. The `Registration` attribute can be either machine or user. The former will create a system DSN record that can be accessed by all users on the computer:

```
<ODBCDataSource Id="OdbcDataSource_MySqlDataSource"
                DriverName="SQL Server"
                Registration="machine"
                KeyPath="yes"
                Name="MySqlDataSource" >
```

Some attributes of the data source can't be set with the `ODBCDataSource` element alone. For example, we need to define which instance of SQL Server to connect to and which database to use by default. For this, we can nest the `Property` element inside of `ODBCDataSource`. The following properties associate our data source with the `MySqlInstance` SQL Server instance, set the master database as the default to connect to, add a description for the data source, and allow Windows authentication:

```
<Property Id="Server"
        Value="[ComputerName]\MySqlInstance" />
<Property Id="Database"
        Value="master" />
<Property Id="Description"
```

```
            Value="A description about my ODBC data source" />
    <Property Id="Trusted_Connection"
            Value="yes" />
```

If you're curious about where the names of these properties came from and whether there are others you could use, then take a look at the Windows registry. All of the attributes of an ODBC data source can be found under `HKEY_LOCAL_MACHINE\SOFTWARE\Wow6432Node\` `ODBC`. The following screenshot is what is set after running our installer:

Name	Type	Data
(Default)	REG_SZ	(value not set)
Database	REG_SZ	master
Description	REG_SZ	Some description about my ODBC data source
Driver	REG_SZ	C:\Windows\system32\SQLSRV32.dll
LastUser	REG_SZ	SYSTEM
Server	REG_SZ	WIN8_PC\MySqlInstance
Trusted_Connection	REG_SZ	yes

The values listed under the `Name` column can be used as the `Id` attributes of your `Property` elements. Try creating a data source through the **ODBC Data Sources Administrative Tools** window and see what values get set in the registry.

13
Admin Tasks

In this chapter, we will cover the following:

- ▶ Setting an environment variable
- ▶ Creating a scheduled task
- ▶ Defining a new event source for the Windows event viewer
- ▶ Registering a performance counter
- ▶ Adding an exception to the Windows Firewall

Introduction

There are a number of install-time chores that I would categorize as administrative tasks—jobs that set up the user's environment. In this chapter, we'll lump a few of these items together and see how to perform them with WiX. We'll cover the very simple chore of adding an environment variable to more complex jobs such as creating a scheduled task or a performance counter.

Setting an environment variable

Environment variables, which are globally available to any software running on the system, provide a means for storing useful information about your application that the end user might reference—usually on the command-line. For example, you might install a variable that contains the path to your software so that the end user could use it as a shortcut when referencing the executable.

Getting ready

Create a new setup project and name it `EnvironmentVariableInstaller`.

How to do it...

Set an environment variable with the `Environment` element as described in the following steps:

1. Add a `Component` element with its `KeyPath` attribute set to `yes`:

    ```
    <Component Id="cmpEnvironmentVariable"
            Guid="{313075B5-BF2C-4012-9A6E-2F4E2C461306}"
            KeyPath="yes">
    </Component>
    ```

2. Within that component, add an `Environment` element that defines the name and value of the new environment variable. Set `Action` to `set` to overwrite any existing value and `System` to `yes` to add it to the `System` collection of environment variables:

    ```
    <Component ...>
      <Environment Id="myEnvironmentVariable"
                Name="MyVariable"
                Value="some value"
                Action="set"
                System="yes" />
    </Component>
    ```

How it works...

The `Environment` element will add a new environment variable to the end user's computer. We can either install it to the `User` collection of variables, by setting the `System` attribute to `no`, or to the `System` collection by setting `System` to `yes`. We defined the variable's name and value with the `Name` and `Value` attributes. The `Action` attribute, when assigned a value of `set`, will overwrite the variable's current value if it exists. To keep any existing value, set `Action` to `create` instead.

To view environment variables in Windows 8.1, go to **System** | **Advanced System Settings** | **Environment Variables...**. You'll see the list of installed variables, as shown:

There's more...

In our example, we defined a new variable that didn't affect any existing variables. If we wanted to append a value to the end of an existing variable, such as adding the path to our application's executable to the built-in `Path` variable, then we would include the `Part` and `Separator` attributes. `Part` should be set to `last` to append to the end of an existing value. The `Separator` attribute defines the delimiter between values in the variable. The following example adds our install directory to the end of the `Path` variable, separating it with a semicolon:

```
<Environment Id="MyPathVariable"
             Name="Path"
             Value="[INSTALLFOLDER]"
             Action="set"
             System="yes"
             Part="last"
             Separator=";" />
```

Creating a scheduled task

Adding a scheduled task to the system allows us to perform some action, such as running an executable, at a specific time each hour, day, or month. It might be to clean up old log files, check for software updates, or process a batch file. With WiX, we can add a scheduled task at the time of installation and remove it when our software is uninstalled.

In this recipe, we'll add a simple task that calls the calculator program once per day. We'll also include markup to remove the task if the installation should fail, or if the user decides to uninstall our software.

Getting ready

To prepare for this recipe, perform the following steps:

1. Create a new setup project and call it `ScheduledTaskInstaller`.

2. For an installer to succeed, it must install at least one file. Add a text file called `Sample.txt` to the project and then add a `Component` and `File` element to it:

```
<ComponentGroup Id="ProductComponents"
                Directory="INSTALLFOLDER">
  <Component Id="cmpSampleTXT"
             Guid="{B63BA28A-0985-472B-828B-B5BD943D0633}">
    <File Source="Sample.txt" />
  </Component>
</ComponentGroup>
```

How to do it...

Add `CustomAction` elements that call the `schtasks` command-line utility to create a scheduled task during installation. Then, create custom actions to remove the scheduled task during uninstall and rollback:

1. Add a `Directory` element that has `Id` as `SystemFolder`. We must reference this directory when calling the `schtasks` utility in our custom actions:

```
<Directory Id="TARGETDIR" Name="SourceDir">
  <Directory Id="ProgramFilesFolder">
    <Directory Id="INSTALLFOLDER"
               Name="ScheduledTaskInstaller" />
  </Directory>
```

```
        <Directory Id="SystemFolder" />
    </Directory>
```

2. Our scheduled task will run as the `LocalSystem` user. Since NT `AUTHORITY\`
   `SYSTEM` doesn't translate on non-English computers, we can use a property from
   `UtilExtension` to get the localized version of that username. Add a project reference
   to `UtilExtension` and then add the following `PropertyRef` element to get access
   to the localized `LocalSystem` user:

```
<PropertyRef Id="WIX_ACCOUNT_LOCALSYSTEM" />
```

3. Add a `CustomAction` element either inside of the `Product` element or within its
   own fragment. Set its `ExeCommand` attribute to use the `schtasks` command-line
   utility to create a new scheduled task. The following example adds a task that will
   run the calculator program each day at 5 p.m. You will not see it, however, because
   it will run in the background.

```
<CustomAction Id="CreateScheduledTask"
              Directory="SystemFolder"
              ExeCommand="&quot;[SystemFolder]schtasks&quot; /
Create /TN MyTaskName /SC DAILY /ST 17:00 /RU &quot;[WIX_ACCOUNT_
LOCALSYSTEM]&quot; /TR &quot;C:\Windows\System32\calc.exe&quot;"
              Execute="deferred"
              Impersonate="no" />
```

4. So that our custom action is undone if there is an error during installation, add a
   second `CustomAction` element to roll back the first. Its `ExeCommand` will pass
   the `/Delete` argument to the `schtasks` utility:

```
<CustomAction Id="RollbackCreateScheduledTask"
              Directory="SystemFolder"
              ExeCommand="&quot;[SystemFolder]schtasks&quot; /
Delete /TN MyTaskName /F"
              Execute="rollback"
              Impersonate="no" />
```

5. Add a third `CustomAction` element to remove the scheduled task during
   uninstallation. Its `ExeCommand` attribute is the same as our rollback custom action's:

```
<CustomAction Id="RemoveScheduledTask"
              Directory="SystemFolder"
              ExeCommand="&quot;[SystemFolder]schtasks&quot; /
Delete /TN MyTaskName /F"
              Execute="deferred"
              Impersonate="no" />
```

6. Schedule each of the custom actions during `InstallExecuteSequence`. Set their conditions so that the `create` and `rollback` actions are performed during installation and the remove process is run during uninstallation:

```
<InstallExecuteSequence>
    <Custom Action="CreateScheduledTask"
            Before="InstallFinalize">NOT Installed</Custom>
    <Custom Action="RollbackCreateScheduledTask"
            Before="CreateScheduledTask">NOT Installed</Custom>
    <Custom Action="RemoveScheduledTask"
            Before="InstallFinalize">REMOVE ~= "ALL"</Custom>
</InstallExecuteSequence>
```

How it works...

The `schtasks` utility, which is preinstalled on Windows, enables us to create or remove a scheduled task. More information about its parameters can be found at `http://msdn.microsoft.com/en-us/library/windows/desktop/bb736357(v=vs.85).aspx`.

For creating the scheduled task, within the `CustomAction` element's `ExeCommand` attribute, use the `/Create` argument. When removing the task, use the `/Delete` argument. Note that our `create` and `remove` actions have their `Execute` attributes set to `deferred`, whereas the `rollback` action has its `Execute` attribute set to `rollback`.

All three custom actions are added to `InstallExecuteSequence` before the `InstallFinalize` action. The `create` and `rollback` actions have their inner-text conditional statements set to `NOT Installed` so that they'll be executed only during installation. The `remove` action, which should run during uninstallation, has a condition of `REMOVE ~= "ALL"`.

Using the `CustomAction` elements in this way will show the momentary flash of a console window when the `schtasks` utility is called. You can use the `CAQuietExec` action, as described in *Chapter 6, Custom Actions*, to execute a command silently.

After running the installer, you should see our scheduled task listed when you navigate to **Control Panel | Administrative Tools | Task Scheduler | Task Scheduler Library** or type `taskschd.msc` in the **Run** window:

Name	Status	Triggers	Next Run Time	Last Run Time
MyTaskName	Ready	At 5:00 PM every day	11/2/2014 5:00:00 PM	Never
Optimize Start Me...	Disabled	When computer is idle		11/1/2014 4:23:08 PM
User_Feed_Synchr...	Ready	At 10:25 PM every day - ...	11/1/2014 10:25:59 PM	11/1/2014 4:05:21 PM

Defining a new event source for the Windows event viewer

The Windows event viewer is a centralized place where application messages are logged, which system administrators can use to monitor the health of the machine. Registering an event source gives us a chance to store hard-coded, localized strings for our own messages. We can select one programmatically by its associated numeric ID. That way, the messages stay consistent and system administrators have one place to go to, to find them.

In this recipe, we'll create a messages file and store it within a resource DLL. Then, we'll register that file with an event source that's installed to the end user's computer. An application can use this event source to log predefined messages to the event viewer.

Getting ready

Create a Setup project and call it `EventSourceInstaller`.

How to do it...

Add a resource file that defines the messages and categories to display in the Windows event viewer. Then, register it with an `EventSource` element. Follow the given steps.

1. Create a file called `messages.mc`. Inside, we'll define the messages and categories that we'll log in the event viewer when a problem occurs within our application. Each definition ends with a period followed by a new line:

```
;// HEADER SECTION
MessageIdTypedef=DWORD

;// CATEGORY DEFINITIONS
MessageId=1
Language=English
Web service
.

;// MESSAGE DEFINITIONS
MessageId=100
Language=English
Max connections was exceeded.
.

MessageId=101
Language=English
Service utilization: %1
.
```

2. Open the Visual Studio command prompt by finding it within the **Start** menu at **Visual Studio 2013 | Visual Studio Tools | Developer Command Prompt for VS2013**.

3. In the command prompt, navigate to the directory where you created the `messages.mc` file and compile it with **Message Compiler** (`mc.exe`):

```
mc messages.mc
```

4. Convert the output RC file to a RES file with **Resource Compiler** (`rc.exe`):

```
rc messages.rc
```

5. Use the linker to bind the output RES and BIN files into a DLL file:

```
link -dll -noentry messages.res
```

6. Copy the output `messages.dll` to our setup project's directory and add a `Component` element for it within the `Product.wxs` file:

```
<ComponentGroup Id="ProductComponents"
                Directory="INSTALLFOLDER">
  <Component Id="cmpMessagesDLL"
             Guid="{F868FE8E-8F1E-4AEC-82AE-B5AB012E152F}">
    <File Id="fileMessagesDLL" Source="messages.dll" />
  </Component>
</ComponentGroup>
```

7. Add `UtilExtension` to the project by right-clicking on the **References** node in **Solution Explorer** and selecting **Add Reference... | WixUtilExtension.dll | Add | OK**.

8. Add the `UtilExtension` namespace to the `Wix` element:

```
<Wix xmlns="http://schemas.microsoft.com/wix/2006/wi"
xmlns:util="http://schemas.microsoft.com/wix/UtilExtension">
```

9. Add a `Component` element with an `EventSource` element that points to the `messages.dll` `File` element with its `EventMessageFile` and `CategoryMessageFile` attributes:

```
<Component Id="cmpEventSource"
           Guid="{2E5A07EC-914B-454F-98C8-77A5F6073C52}">
  <util:EventSource
    KeyPath="yes"
    EventMessageFile="[#fileMessagesDLL]"
    CategoryMessageFile="[#fileMessagesDLL]"
    CategoryCount="1"
    Name="MyCustomEventSource"
    Log="Application" />
</Component>
```

How it works...

A message file defines localizable strings that are tied to numeric IDs. Within our software, we can choose which message to show in the Windows event log based on one of these IDs. For example, to display the error, **Max connections was exceeded**, we could call the `WriteEvent` static method on the `System.Diagnostics.EventLog` class, passing in an instance of `EventInstance`. The `EventInstance` class constructor takes the message ID as its first parameter, the category ID as its second, and an optional `EventLogEntryType` to log the message at a certain severity level:

```
EventLog.WriteEvent(
    "MyCustomEventSource",
    new EventInstance(100, 1, EventLogEntryType.Error));
```

Since we passed 1 for the category parameter, the new event will be grouped within the web service category as defined in our `messages.mc` file. Open the event viewer by typing `eventvwr` in the **Run** window. Here's an example of what our message would look like:

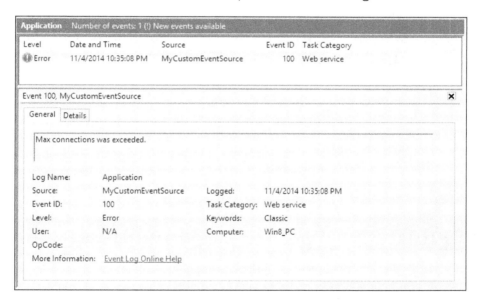

The strings in the message file can also accept placeholders as follows:

```
MessageId=101
Language=English
Service utilization: %1
.
```

The `WriteEvent` method will accept an optional third parameter to fill in the placeholder:

```
EventLog.WriteEvent(
  "MyCustomEventSource",
  new EventInstance(101, 1, EventLogEntryType.Information),
  "75 percent");
```

In the event log, we'll see the message **Service utilization: 75 percent**. More information about how to format message files can be found at `http://msdn.microsoft.com/en-us/library/windows/desktop/dd996906(v=vs.85).aspx`.

To install our event source and its associated resource file, we added `messages.dll` to a component so that it would be copied to the end user's computer. Next, we referenced `UtilExtension` to get access to its `EventSource` element. The `EventSource` element's `EventMessageFile` and `CategoryMessageFile` attributes point to the files that contain our messages and categories. They can point to separate files, but in our case, we stored our categories and messages all in one. `CategoryCount` is simply a count of the number of categories in our file. The `Name` attribute gives our event source a name that we can reference in our code. The log groups it with other similar events.

After installation, we can verify that our event source was added by opening the Windows registry and looking for the `HKEY_LOCAL_MACHINE\SYSTEM\CurrentControlSet\Services\EventLog\Application\MyCustomEventSource` key. There you'll find the values that we set on the `EventSource` element:

Name	Type	Data
(Default)	REG_SZ	(value not set)
CategoryCount	REG_DWORD	0x00000001 (1)
CategoryMessageFile	REG_EXPAND_SZ	C:\Program Files (x86)\EventSourceInstaller\messages.dll
EventMessageFile	REG_EXPAND_SZ	C:\Program Files (x86)\EventSourceInstaller\messages.dll

Registering a performance counter

When trying to diagnose the health or performance of an application, there's usually never enough information. It's always nice to provide more. Performance counters allow us to continuously log the current state of our software and, with the help of tools like Performance Monitor that are baked into Windows, provide a standard view of that data for system administrators.

In this recipe, we'll add a new performance counter for logging the number of sandwiches made for a school lunch program. We'll use Performance Monitor to see a live feed of this data as it occurs. We'll write a simple console application to publish the sandwich count.

Getting ready

To prepare for this recipe, we'll install a test console application along with our performance counter so that we can enter data and see it displayed in the Performance Monitor in real time. Follow these steps to include the test app in our installer:

1. Create a new setup project and call it `PerformanceCounterInstaller`.

2. Within the same Visual Studio solution, add a C# Console Application project and add the following code to its `Program.cs` file:

```
using System;
using System.Diagnostics;

namespace LunchPerformanceTestApp
{
  public class Program
  {
    const string perfCategory = "Lunch Counters";
    const string perfCounterName = "Sandwich Count";

    public static void Main(string[] args)
    {
      PerformanceCounter counter = null;

      if (PerformanceCounterCategory.Exists(perfCategory))
      {
        counter = new PerformanceCounter(
                  perfCategory,
                  perfCounterName,
                  false);

        while (true)
        {
          Console.WriteLine("Enter number of sandwiches to make
(or 'q' to quit): ");
```

```
            string userInput = Console.ReadLine();

            if (userInput == "q")
            {
              break;
            }

            long numberOfSandwiches;
            if (long.TryParse(
                  userInput,
                  out numberOfSandwiches))
            {
              counter.RawValue = numberOfSandwiches;
            }
          }
        }
        else
        {
          Console.WriteLine("Performance Category not found.");
        }

        Console.ReadKey();
      }
    }
  }
```

3. Add the console application as a reference in the
    `PerformanceCounterInstaller` project and add a `Component` and `File`
    element to include it in the installer:

```
<Component Id="cmpLunchPerformanceTestAppEXE"
           Guid="{B9FC6F0A-6D21-41F8-B2EA-951AD4FAA9CE}">
  <File
Source="$(var.LunchPerformanceTestApp.TargetDir)
LunchPerformanceTestApp.exe" />
</Component>
```

How to do it...

Add `PerformanceCategory` with child `PerformanceCounter` elements to set up a
new category with counters that can be viewed in the Windows Performance Monitor:

1. Add the `UtilExtension` namespace to the project by right-clicking on the **References** node in **Solution Explorer** and selecting **Add Reference... | WixUtilExtension.dll | Add | OK**.

2. Add the `UtilExtension` namespace to the `Wix` element:

```
<Wix xmlns="http://schemas.microsoft.com/wix/2006/wi"
xmlns:util="http://schemas.microsoft.com/wix/UtilExtension">
```

3. Add a `Component` element with its `KeyPath` attribute set to `yes`:

```
<Component Id="cmpPerformanceCounter"
          Guid="{D38B14AE-782E-491E-BE6F-197627BA3C29}"
          KeyPath="yes">
</Component>
```

4. Within that component, add a `PerformanceCategory` element that assigns a name to our new category:

```
<Component ...>
  <util:PerformanceCategory Id="sandwichCategory"
                            Name="Lunch Counters"
                            Help="Logging of lunch data">
  </util:PerformanceCategory>
</Component>
```

5. Within `PerformanceCategory`, add one or more `PerformanceCounter` elements that will define the names and data types of counters within the category:

```
<util:PerformanceCategory ...>
  <util:PerformanceCounter Name="Sandwich Count"
                           Type="numberOfItems64"
                           Help="Number of sandwiches made" />
</util:PerformanceCategory>
```

How it works...

The `PerformanceCategory` element from `UtilExtension` gives us the ability to define new performance categories that contain one or more counters. Any `PerformanceCounter` elements that we add within it can be used by our applications to log real-time data points. Each counter is given a data type via its `Type` attribute. We have many data types to choose from. An explanation of each can be found at `http://msdn.microsoft.com/en-us/library/system.diagnostics.performancecountertype(v=vs.90).aspx`. In this case, we chose to make it the `numberOfItems64` type, which in C# is `long`.

After running the installer, we can start the Performance Monitor by opening the **Run** window and typing `perfmon`. In its left-hand panel, right-click on the **Performance Monitor** node under the `Monitoring Tools` folder and then select **New Window from Here**. This will bring up a window that doesn't have any counters added to it yet:

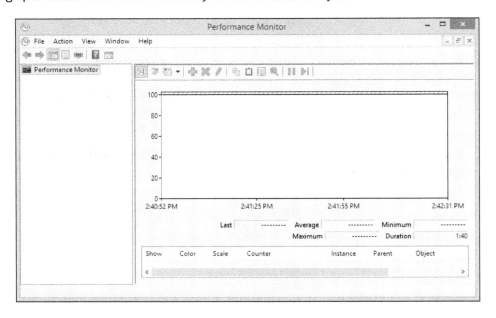

Click the green **+** icon and scroll to the **Lunch Counters** category. Expand it, highlight **Sandwich Count**, and then click on **Add >>** | **OK**, as follows:

Then, navigate to our install directory and launch the `LunchPerformanceTestApp` console application. It will ask you to enter a number. Each time that you do, it will be displayed in the Performance Monitor, as shown in the following screenshot:

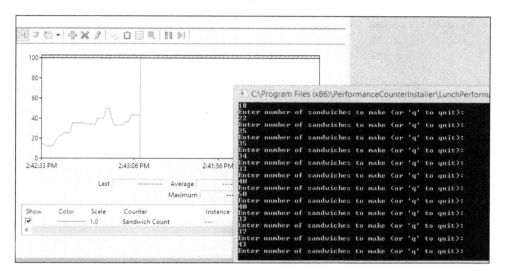

Adding an exception to Windows Firewall

Windows Firewall protects us from hackers that might try to connect to random ports on our computer. However, if we want to allow our own programs to receive messages, we'll need to add exceptions to the firewall to let them through. In this recipe, we'll install a console application that listens on a certain port and then add this program to the list of applications that are allowed to have incoming messages pass through the firewall.

Getting ready

So that we're able to test our firewall exception, let's create a console application that will listen on a TCP port. Ordinarily, if anyone on a different computer tried to access that port to send a request, it would be blocked by the firewall. Perform the following steps to set up the application and include it in our installer:

1. Create a new C# Console Application project named `PortListeningProgram` and add the following code to its `Program.cs` file:

    ```
    using System;
    using System.IO;
    using System.Net;
    using System.Net.Sockets;
    using System.Text;
    ```

```
using System.Threading;

namespace PortListeningProgram
{
  public class Program
  {
    public static void Main(string[] args)
    {
      Console.WriteLine("Listening for incoming requests...");

      int port = 50000;
      IPEndPoint endpoint = new IPEndPoint(
                                IPAddress.Any,
                                port);

      TcpListener listener = new TcpListener(endpoint);
      listener.Start();

      while(true)
      {
        Thread.Sleep(10);

        // A client is connecting...
        using (TcpClient client = listener.AcceptTcpClient())
        {
          NetworkStream stream = client.GetStream();
          string helloMessage = "Connected to program. Type a
message to send...\n";

          stream.Write(
            Encoding.UTF8.GetBytes(helloMessage),
            0,
            helloMessage.Length);

          byte[] receivedBytes = new byte[128];

          // until they disconnect, print their messages
          while (client.Connected)
          {
            try
            {
```

```
                    Array.Clear(
                      receivedBytes,
                      0,
                      receivedBytes.Length);

                    stream.Read(
                      receivedBytes,
                      0,
                      receivedBytes.Length);

                    Console.WriteLine(
                      Encoding.UTF8.GetString(receivedBytes));
                  }
                  catch (IOException)
                  {
                    Console.WriteLine("Client disconnected.");
                  }
                }
              }
            }
          }
        }
}
```

2. Add a setup project to the same solution and call it FirewallExceptionInstaller.

3. Within the setup project, add PortListeningProgram as a project reference and then add a Component and File element to include it in the installer:

```
<ComponentGroup Id="ProductComponents"
                Directory="INSTALLFOLDER">
  <Component Id="cmpPortListeningProgramEXE"
             Guid="{BD7507FB-083F-498B-95C4-F599433A2FD6}">
    <File Id="filePortListeningProgram"
Source="$(var.PortListeningProgram.TargetDir)PortListeningProgram.
exe" />
  </Component>
</ComponentGroup>
```

How to do it...

Use the `FirewallException` element from `FirewallExtension` to allow connections through the Windows Firewall:

1. Add `FirewallExtension` to the project by right-clicking on the **References** node in **Solution Explorer** and selecting **Add Reference...** | **WixFirewallExtension.dll** | **Add** | **OK**.

2. Add the `FirewallExtension` namespace to the `Wix` element:

   ```
   <Wix xmlns="http://schemas.microsoft.com/wix/2006/wi"
   xmlns:fw="http://schemas.microsoft.com/wix/FirewallExtension">
   ```

3. Add a component that contains a `FirewallException` element that will allow our program to receive incoming requests through the firewall:

   ```
   <Component Id="cmpFirewallException"
              Guid="{DB1A8DBF-47DE-40DC-A5A2-3E08ECBA5D5B}"
              KeyPath="yes">
     <fw:FirewallException Id="MyFirewallException"
                           Program="[#filePortListeningProgram]"
                           Description="Lets requests through"
                           Name="My Firewall Exception"
                           Scope="any"
                           Protocol="tcp" />
   </Component>
   ```

How it works...

We started off by building a console application that will accept incoming requests on TCP port `50000`. Although the Windows Firewall will typically allow any outgoing messages to pass through without any interference, it blocks any incoming messages unless an exception is made for that port or the program that listens on that port. So by default, our application will be cut off from the outside world.

To remedy this situation, we referenced `FirewallExtension` that ships with the WiX Toolset and added a `FirewallException` element to our setup project. `FirewallException` takes either a `Port` or `Program` attribute to know what to add an exception for. In our example, we chose the latter, giving it the path to our `PortListeningProgram` console application. The `Description` and `Name` attributes show up in the Windows Firewall control panel, which you can see by opening the **Run** window and typing `wf.msc`. Select the **Inbound Rules** node to see that our new firewall exception has been added:

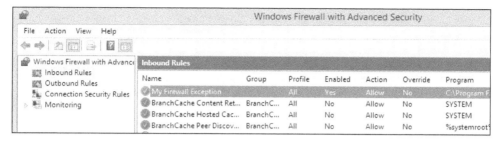

The `FirewallException` element's `Scope` attribute indicates whether incoming requests can come from just our local network—with a value of `localSubnet`—or the entire Internet—with a value of `any`. The `Protocol` attribute is set to `tcp` to designate that our application has opened a TCP port, although it can alternatively be set to `udp` to add an exception for a UDP port.

If we fire up the console application that we've installed, it will begin listening for incoming requests on TCP port `50000`. We can then send messages to that port from outside the firewall, or in other words, from a different computer, as shown in the following screenshot:

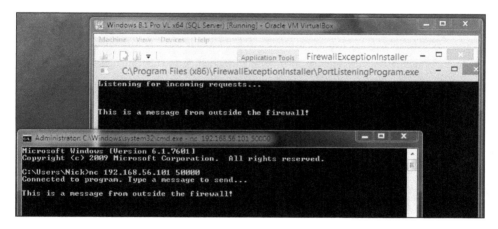

Here, I'm using Oracle's VirtualBox, available at `https://www.virtualbox.org`, to set up a virtual machine running Windows 8.1. I've set the virtual machine up with host-only networking so that it has an IP address that is accessible from the host. Then, using Netcat for Windows, which can be downloaded from `http://joncraton.org/blog/46/netcat-for-windows`, I've sent a message to port `50000` on the virtual machine. I've used the following Netcat command:

```
nc 192.168.56.101 50000
```

Whatever I type next will be immediately displayed on the other end in our `PortListeningProgram` console application's window. This tells us that our firewall exception is working, allowing messages to pass through.

Index

Thank you for buying
WiX Cookbook

About Packt Publishing

Packt, pronounced 'packed', published its first book, *Mastering phpMyAdmin for Effective MySQL Management*, in April 2004, and subsequently continued to specialize in publishing highly focused books on specific technologies and solutions.

Our books and publications share the experiences of your fellow IT professionals in adapting and customizing today's systems, applications, and frameworks. Our solution-based books give you the knowledge and power to customize the software and technologies you're using to get the job done. Packt books are more specific and less general than the IT books you have seen in the past. Our unique business model allows us to bring you more focused information, giving you more of what you need to know, and less of what you don't.

Packt is a modern yet unique publishing company that focuses on producing quality, cutting-edge books for communities of developers, administrators, and newbies alike. For more information, please visit our website at www.packtpub.com.

About Packt Open Source

In 2010, Packt launched two new brands, Packt Open Source and Packt Enterprise, in order to continue its focus on specialization. This book is part of the Packt open source brand, home to books published on software built around open source licenses, and offering information to anybody from advanced developers to budding web designers. The Open Source brand also runs Packt's open source Royalty Scheme, by which Packt gives a royalty to each open source project about whose software a book is sold.

Writing for Packt

We welcome all inquiries from people who are interested in authoring. Book proposals should be sent to author@packtpub.com. If your book idea is still at an early stage and you would like to discuss it first before writing a formal book proposal, then please contact us; one of our commissioning editors will get in touch with you.

We're not just looking for published authors; if you have strong technical skills but no writing experience, our experienced editors can help you develop a writing career, or simply get some additional reward for your expertise.

WiX: A Developer's Guide to Windows Installer XML

ISBN: 978-1-84951-372-2   Paperback: 348 pages

Create a hassle-free installer for your Windows software using WIX

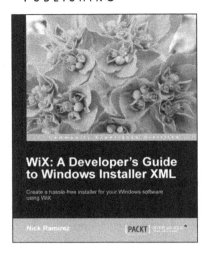

1. Package your software into a single MSI file for easy installation.

2. Read and write to Windows Registry and create, start, and stop Windows Services during installation.

3. Write .NET code that performs specific tasks during installation via custom actions.

4. Learn how the WiX command-line tools work to build and link your project.

WiX 3.6: A Developer's Guide to Windows Installer XML

ISBN: 978-1-78216-042-7   Paperback: 488 pages

An in-and-out, to-the-point introduction to Windows Installer XML

1. Brings the reader up to speed on all of the major features of WiX, including the new bootstrapper engine, Burn.

2. Provides a richer understanding of the underlying Windows Installer technology.

3. Showcases the flexibility and versatility of WiX, with a few tips and tricks along the way.

Please check **www.PacktPub.com** for information on our titles

www.ingramcontent.com/pod-product-compliance
Lightning Source LLC
Chambersburg PA
CBHW060537060326
40690CB00017B/3523